STRANGE FACTS,
BIZARRE CUSTOMS,
INCREDIBLE EVENTS–

collected from all over the world by the tireless Ripley's staff and vividly illustrated in this amazing new book.

If you cannot find your favorite **Believe It or Not!** POCKET BOOK at your local newsstand, please write to the nearest Ripley's "Believe It or Not!" museum:

175 Jefferson Street, San Francisco, California 94133

1500 North Wells Street, Chicago, Illinois 60610

19 San Marco Avenue, St. Augustine, Florida 32084

The Parkway
Gatlinburg, Tennessee 37738

145 East Elkhorn Avenue, Estes Park, Colorado 80517

4960 Clifton Hill, Niagara Falls, Canada

Central Promenade, Blackpool, Lancashire, England

Ripley's Believe It or Not! titles

Ripley's Believe It or Not! 2nd Series
Ripley's Believe It or Not! 3rd Series
Ripley's Believe It or Not! 4th Series
Ripley's Believe It or Not! 5th Series
Ripley's Believe It or Not! 6th Series
Ripley's Believe It or Not! 7th Series
Ripley's Believe It or Not! 8th Series
Ripley's Believe It or Not! 9th Series
Ripley's Believe It or Not! 10th Series
Ripley's Believe It or Not! 11th Series
Ripley's Believe It or Not! 12th Series
Ripley's Believe It or Not! 13th Series
Ripley's Believe It or Not! 14th Series
Ripley's Believe It or Not! 15th Series
Ripley's Believe It or Not! 16th Series
Ripley's Believe It or Not! 17th Series
Ripley's Believe It or Not! 18th Series
Ripley's Believe It or Not! 19th Series
Ripley's Believe It or Not! 20th Series
Ripley's Believe It or Not! 21st Series
Ripley's Believe It or Not! 22nd Series
Ripley's Believe It or Not! 23rd Series
Ripley's Believe It or Not! 24th Series
Ripley's Believe It or Not! 25th Series
Ripley's Believe It or Not! 26th Series
Ripley's Believe It or Not! Anniversary Edition
Ripley's Believe It or Not! Book of Americana
Ripley's Believe It or Not! Book of the Military
Ripley's Believe It or Not! Book of Undersea Oddities

Published by POCKET BOOKS

Ripley's Believe It or Not!

26th Series

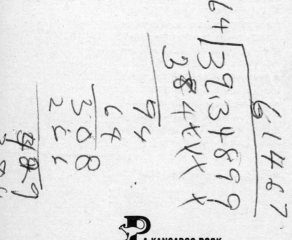

A KANGAROO BOOK

PUBLISHED BY POCKET BOOKS NEW YORK

RIPLEY'S BELIEVE IT OR NOT!® 26TH SERIES

POCKET BOOK edition published August, 1977

This original POCKET BOOK edition is printed
from brand-new plates.
POCKET BOOK editions are published by
POCKET BOOKS,
a Simon & Schuster Division of
GULF & WESTERN CORPORATION
1230 Avenue of the Americas,
New York, N.Y. 10020.
Trademarks registered in the United States
and other countries.

PREFACE

In parts of Europe it is considered unlucky to cut one's fingernails on a Sunday. According to a Devonshire rhyme, "He who on the Sabbath pares his horn, 'twere better for him he had ne'er been born." In other places it was once considered unlucky to shave the beard on a Sunday, and if a feather bed were "turned" on a Sunday, it was most unfortunate.

Sunday is not without its share of weather lore either: "Rain a'fore church, rain all week," and "If it rains on a Sunday before mess (Mass), it will rain all the week more or less."

You should also be careful when you sneeze on a Sunday. In Hertfordshire, England, they say that "Sneeze on a Sunday and the Devil will have dominion over you all week." In many places it is held that a sneeze before Sunday breakfast means that "you will see your true love before the week is past."

From Cornwall, England, we hear that "Sunday's child is full of grace," and in many other cultures Sunday's child has been singled out as possessing special birth rights. In early times it was claimed that Sunday children were safe from the "evil eye." In Germany they were regarded as privileged beings, and in Denmark they were thought to have the faculty of seeing things hidden from others. In Transylvania, too, only a child born on a Sunday could see the bluish flame that reveals the presence of buried treasure.

In East Anglia, England, Sunday was regarded as a day for good beginnings, and the mother of a newborn child would walk downstairs on a Sunday if it was at all possible.

"Never in a month of Sundays" is a phrase commonly used today but we are not sure where it originated. Perhaps it comes from the Yorkshire saying, "Tomorrow come never, when two Sundays come together"—which brings us to the point of all this. This book is literally filled with *a month of Sundays:* in fact, many months of Sundays.

Since King Features Syndicate started carrying Robert Ripley's *Believe It or Not* column in 1929, not a single day has passed in which a Ripley cartoon did not appear in the newspapers. With four to six items featured in every cartoon, this adds up to hundreds of thousands of Ripley oddities that, sooner or later, have found their way into one of the twenty-five in the series of Pocket Books that the Ripley organization has published over the years. All, that is, *but the Sunday features.* For some reason, perhaps because of their unusually large size, most of these cartoons have escaped publication in book form. We felt this was unfortunate: considering the additional numbers of readers we have on Sundays, the illustrations are often printed in color. Consequently, many of our best oddities have appeared in these Sunday editions. So for this volume we have gone back as far as 1929 and chosen several hundred of our "Sunday Best." We are sure readers will agree that they make good reading any day of the week.

—Derek R. Copperthwaite,
Research Director,
BELIEVE IT OR NOT!

Ripley's Believe It or Not!

26th Series

THE REWARDS OF HONESTY!

SIR WILLIAM PHIPS (1651-1695) WHO STARTED HIS CAREER AS A SHEPHERD IN MAINE, LOCATED A $1,500,000 SUNKEN TREASURE IN 1687 AND TURNED OVER *ALL BUT $80,000 OF IT TO HIS FINANCIAL BACKERS* –

HIS HONESTY SO IMPRESSED KING JAMES II THAT PHIPS WAS KNIGHTED AND MADE GOVERNOR OF MASSACHUSETTS--WHICH THEN INCLUDED MAINE, NOVA SCOTIA, CONNECTICUT AND RHODE ISLAND

THE CROWN

WORN BY KING MONGKUT of SIAM (1804-1868) IS A HEADPIECE KNOWN AS THE "MONGKUT" IN HIS HONOR AND THE *OFFICIAL SYMBOL OF THAILAND*

2 POTATOES

ONE SHAPED LIKE A DOVE AND THE OTHER A BUFFALO *THAT GREW SIDE BY SIDE*

Submitted by Steve Kerro Indianapolis, Ind.

STONES MARKED BY NATURE WITH *CHINESE RELIGIOUS SYMBOLS*

Submitted by Hyatte L. Tomer Grover City, Calif.

THE COAT OF ARMS

OF SIMANCAS, SPAIN, FEATURES THE RIGHT HANDS OF 7 GIRLS WHO WHEN TAKEN CAPTIVE BY THE MOORS *CUT OFF THEIR RIGHT HANDS RATHER THAN SURRENDER TO THEIR MASTERS*

THE SILK COTTON TREE

PRODUCES ITS ATTRACTIVE CRIMSON FLOWERS *BEFORE IT GROWS LEAVES*

ALFRED SÖRENSEN, a Dane, BECAME AN INDIAN HOLY MAN, AND LIVED IN A RETREAT IN THE HIMALAYAS *FOR 22 YEARS*

THE **VIRGINIA DAY FLOWER** IS SO NAMED BECAUSE IT BLOOMS *FOR ONLY ONE DAY*

THE **CATHEDRAL OF ZAGREB** Yugoslavia, BEGUN IN THE 13TH CENTURY, WAS COMPLETED *5 CENTURIES LATER*

THE **SIEGE** THAT WAS WON BY GENEROUS SERVINGS OF WINE!

THURANDT CASTLE ON A MOUNTAIN OVERLOOKING ALKEN, GERMANY, DEFEATED A 2-YEAR SIEGE BY ROLLING DOWN THE STEEP SLOPE, **6,000 HUGE CASKS OF WINE.** THE BESIEGING TROOPS DRANK SO MUCH THAT THEY BECAME BEFUDDLED AND ABANDONED THE SIEGE (1246-1248)

A SUNDIAL IN THE RAGIONE PALACE IN BERGAMO, ITALY, CONSISTS MERELY OF A LINE ON THE FLOOR ON WHICH THE HOUR IS INDICATED BY *A GNOMON LOCATED IN THE CEILING*

A **CHARM** WORN IN TURKEY AS PROTECTION AGAINST EVIL CONSISTS OF THE HORNS OF A STAG BEETLE, A COIN *AND A BLUE GLASS EYE*

A **SILVER CONTAINER** IN THE FORM OF A BUST OF SAINT MARINO, IN THE BASILICA OF SAN MARINO, IN THE REPUBLIC NAMED FOR THE SAINT, *CONTAINS THE SAINT'S SKULL*

EMPRESS CATHERINE I (1683-1727) of Russia, COULD NOT READ OR WRITE. *SHE LEARNED TO SIGN HER NAME ONLY AFTER SHE BECAME RULER AT THE AGE OF 41*

THE **CHURN GEYSER** in Iceland, WHICH HURLS A COLUMN OF BOILING WATER 100 FEET INTO THE AIR FOR AS LONG AS 15 MINUTES, IS ACTIVATED BY TOSSING INTO ITS CIRCULAR OPENING *A WHEEL-BARROW-LOAD OF DIRT*

TOMBSTONE in Wolfershausen, Germany, ERECTED BY THE WIDOW BIERMANN OVER THE GRAVES OF HER 2 CARRIAGE HORSES —WHICH SHE HAD ORDERED *SHOT RATHER THAN RETIRE THEM TO PASTURE*

HERE LIE BELLA AND ROSE JUNE 10, 1868

THE **MAN** WHO LIVED UP TO HIS NAME! **ROBERT VERNON** (1854-1911) OF PARIS, FRANCE, LIVED FOR 3 YEARS IN EACH OF THESE 12 COUNTRIES:

RUSSIA **V**ENEZUELA
ORKNEYS **E**CUADOR
BRAZIL **R**YUKYU
EGYPT **N**ICARAGUA
RUMANIA **O**MAN
TUNISIA **N**EW ZEALAND

THEIR INITIALS SPELL HIS NAME

THE **CHURCH OF VOROBLEVYCHI** IN THE UKRAINE, IS LOCATED IN *A HOLLOW TREE TRUNK*

THE WOMAN WHO GAVE HER LIFE TO SAVE A COMPLETE STRANGER!
Madame Maillé

A PRISONER IN THE FRENCH REVOLUTIONARY PRISON OF LA CONCIERGERIE IN 1793 WAS SAVED WHEN A GUARD CALLED HER TO ENTER A GUILLOTINE-BOUND TUMBRIL, BECAUSE AN ARISTOCRAT NAMED MADAME MAILLET--WHOSE NAME WAS PRONOUNCED LIKE THAT OF MADAME MAILLÉ--TOOK HER PLACE.
MADAME MAILLET HAD LEARNED THAT MADAME MAILLÉ WAS THE MOTHER OF 8 CHILDREN

THE MAORI WOMAN
near Whitianga, N.Z.
NATURAL ROCK FORMATION

THE BRONZE DOOR
of Castel Nuovo, Naples, Italy,
STILL HAS EMBEDDED IN IT
A CANNONBALL FIRED DURING
A SIEGE **478** YEARS AGO

THE **DOLGANS**
of Siberia,
LIVE IN WINTER
IN A SMALL
WOODEN HUT
*MOUNTED ON
A SLED*

**THE SKINS OF
WHITE HORSES**

ARE SUSPENDED BY OSTIAKS OF SIBERIA
*TO GUARD THEIR VILLAGE
FROM EVIL SPIRITS*

ST. EDWARD RINGS
WERE GOLD OR
SILVER RINGS
GIVEN TO FRIENDS
BY ENGLISH KINGS
--WITH THEIR BLESSINGS--
IN THE 18th CENTURY, AS
A CURE FOR CRAMPS

15 WHALING SHIPS
LOADED WITH ROCKS AT NEW BEDFORD, MASS., WERE
SUNK IN THE CHANNELS OF THE HARBORS OF
CHARLESTON AND SAVANNAH IN 1861 BY THE UNION
FORCES TO PREVENT *CONFEDERATE BLOCKADE RUNNING*

A GANNET
CAN BREATHE IN 3 TIMES
AS MUCH AIR AS A MAN

SILVER COINS
MINTED IN ULM,
GERMANY, IN 1704,
WERE SQUARE

THE OLDEST SEAGOING BOAT
A VESSEL 46 FEET LONG
AND ROWED BY 20 MEN.
IT WAS FOUND NEAR ALSEN, DENMARK,
AND WAS CONSTRUCTED ABOUT *500 B.C.*

ARROWHEADS ARE MADE BY NATIVES OF GAUA, NEW HEBRIDES, *FROM THE SHARP SPINES OF THE STINGRAY*

THE **MAN** WHOSE NAME WAS A PROPHECY OF HIS DEATH!
FRANZ BIENSTOCK (1766-1870) of Berlin, Germany, WHOSE LAST NAME IS GERMAN FOR A HIVE, *WAS STUNG TO DEATH AT THE AGE OF 104 BY A SWARM OF BEES*

THE **BISCUIT SEASTAR** OF AUSTRALIA, BEARS AN AMAZING RESEMBLANCE *TO A BISCUIT*

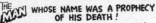

THE STERN MARQUISE near Signes, France, NATURAL STONE FORMATION

THE SPHINX ROCK ELCHO ISLAND, AUSTRALIA, *NATURAL STONE FORMATION*

WILLIE MARSHALL 1872-1944
HIS WIFE DELLA 1876
SHE ALWAYS DID HER BEST
HE NEVER DID

GRAVESTONE IN HARDWICK, VERMONT

THE **GREAT SILVER BEETLE** IS A VEGETARIAN --YET ITS LARVA *IS CARNIVOROUS*

THE **THE OLDEST KNOWN HAT** FOUND AT SCHIFFERSTADT, GERMANY, AND DATING TO THE 12th CENTURY, B.C., IS SOLID GOLD

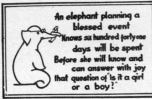

An elephant planning a blessed event
Knows six hundred fortyone
days will be spent
Before she will know and
can answer with joy
that question of 'Is it a girl
or a boy?'

TABLET IN THE ELEPHANT HOUSE OF THE ZOO AT COLOMBO, CEYLON --*GIVING ITS INFORMATION IN RHYME*

LORD CASTLEREAGH (1769-1822) WHO LATER BECAME A FAMOUS BRITISH STATESMAN, WON HIS FIRST ELECTION TO PARLIAMENT FROM COUNTY DOWN, IRELAND, BY SPENDING 60,000 POUNDS-- THE EQUIVALENT TODAY OF **$6,000,000.** *THE ELECTION IMPOV- ERISHED HIS FATHER*

THE **BRITISH EMBASSY** IN ISTANBUL, TURKEY, BUILT BY AN ENGLISHMAN IN 1843, IS A REPLICA *OF THE BARBARINI PALACE IN ROME, ITALY*

FRANÇOIS CHICOYNEAU (1672-1752) CHANCELLOR OF THE UNIVERSITY of Montpellier, France, PRACTICED MEDICINE FOR 59 YEARS *WITHOUT EVER CHARGING A FEE*

GYNANDROMORPH A SPECIES OF ANT *IS HALF MALE AND HALF FEMALE*

ROOFS OF HOMES IN THE HIGH CHANG PLATEAU IN CAMEROON, AFRICA, CONSIST OF BANG PALM BRANCHES TIED WITH BARK SO SMOOTHLY THE BUILDERS CAN SWARM OVER A ROOF WITHOUT ENCOUNTERING *A SINGLE SHARP PROJECTION* ···

THE **MAN** WHO CONSUMED 16,071 BANQUETS TO CELEBRATE ONE EVENT!
THE **DUKE de HUMIÈRES** (1628-1694) WAS MADE A FIELD MARSHAL IN 1650, AND BECAUSE THE NUMERALS IN THAT YEAR ADD UP TO 12, HE ATE A DINNER OF 12 COURSES EACH NIGHT FOR 44 YEARS·· CHANGING HIS ATTIRE COMPLETELY BEFORE EACH COURSE

CASPAR MATHER
TSIMPSHEAN INDIAN OF KETCHIKAN, ALASKA -- STILL CARVED TOTEM POLES *AT THE AGE OF 95* !
Submitted by Emery F. Tobin Vancouver, Wash.

WHALERS' GRAVES IN NEW ZEALAND WERE OFTEN MARKED *BY AN UPTURNED WHALING CANOE*

THE **ELEPHANT FISH** of Africa COMMUNICATE WITH EACH OTHER *BY AN ELECTRICAL IMPULSE*

THE **TOWN HALL** of Filsen, Germany,
IS LOCATED
ABOVE A GATE IN THE TOWN WALL

THE **CHURCH BELL**
OF MANY CHURCHES
IN ETHIOPIA, IS A BLOCK
OF BASALT ROCK

A **HOUSE** IN MASITISI, BASUTOLAND,
SO. AFRICA --*BUILT INSIDE A CAVE*

THE TIBETAN BIBLE
CONSISTING OF **108** VOLUMES
WITH RAISED GOLDEN LETTERS,
WAS BEGUN IN 1436 AND NOT COM-
PLETED UNTIL 1447, *11 YEARS LATER*

**CHINESE
SYMBOL**
FOR
"GUARANTEE"
IS A COMBINATION
OF THE SYMBOLS
FOR "STUPID"
AND " MAN "

HERE LIES THE BODY OF OUR ANNA
DONE TO DEATH BY A BANANA
IT WASN'T THE FRUIT
THAT LAID HER LOW
BUT THE SKIN OF THE THING
THAT MADE HER GO

Epitaph OF ANNA HOPEWELL
IN ENOSBURG, VERMONT

*ROBERT
WALKER*

(1709-1802)
SERVED AS
A MINISTER
IN Buttermere,
England,
*CONTINUOUSLY
FOR 67 YEARS*

THE GOVERNMENT HOUSE
IN AUCKLAND, N.Z., WAS BUILT IN ENGLAND IN 1840,
*THEN DISMANTLED AND SHIPPED BY BOAT TO NEW ZEALAND WHERE
IT SERVED AS A RESIDENCE OF THE GOVERNOR FOR 8 YEARS*

THE SEA CHAPEL OF LA BERNERIE France, CONSTRUCTED IN 1405, *WAS SWEPT AWAY BY THE SEA IN 1860*

A **NECKLACE** MADE FROM THE RAREST OF ENAMELS --*CIRCULAR TEETH FROM UNIQUE MICE*-- WAS GIVEN TO FRIENDS BY THE EMPEROR OF ETHIOPIA *AS A REMEDY FOR CROSSED EYES*

THE **BLUE-WINGED GOOSE** IS FOUND NO-WHERE IN THE WORLD EXCEPT *IN THE HIGHLANDS OF ETHIOPIA*

THE **NATIONAL FLAG** OF THE ANCIENT MAORIS OF NEW ZEALAND --*LONG BEFORE THE ARRIVAL OF THE FIRST EUROPEAN*-- FEATURED THE CHRISTIAN CROSS AS WELL AS THE MUSLIM STAR AND CRESCENT

THE **MOST AMAZING PLEA FOR COMPASSION IN ALL HISTORY!** MADAME THERESE TALLIEN (1773- 1835) ABOUT TO GIVE BIRTH WHEN SHE LEARNED A CLOSE FAMILY FRIEND, THE COUNT DE SENONVILLE, WAS ON HIS WAY TO THE GUILLOTINE, *DRESSED, ORDERED HER CARRIAGE AND CALLED ON NAPOLEON TO PLEAD FOR MERCY.* THE COUNT WAS REPRIEVED AND MADAME TALLIEN NAMED HER BABY GIRL CLEMENCE--IN COMMEMORATION OF THE GRANT OF CLEMENCY (FEBRUARY 1, 1800)

"SUEDE" THE PET CAT OF MRS. ROSE SOLAKIAN OF BURBANK, CALIFORNIA, REGULARLY NIPS ROSES FROM THE GARDEN AND DROPS THEM AT HER OWNER'S FEET

RAINBOW VIOLETS

VIOLETS PRODUCING FLOWERS THAT ARE *YELLOW, PURPLE AND BLUE*

SIR **John PRYCE** of Haverfordwest, Wales, KEPT THE EMBALMED BODIES OF HIS FIRST TWO WIVES IN *GRANDFATHER'S CLOCKS BESIDE HIS BED.*

THEY WERE BURIED ONLY WHEN THE WOMAN HE CHOSE TO BE HIS THIRD WIFE REFUSED TO SHARE THE BEDROOM WITH THE CORPSES OF HER PREDECESSORS

THE **2-FACED CAT** A KITTEN BORN *WITH 4 EYES, 2 NOSES AND 2 MOUTHS* --ALL OF WHICH FUNCTIONED Submitted by Billy J. Broussard, Vinton, La.

BRASS BATTLE HELMETS ARE WORN BY THE TOBELAS OF CENTRAL CELEBES, INDONESIA, AS REGULAR HEADGEAR *--SYMBOLS OF BRAVERY BECAUSE THEY WERE WORN BY DUTCH CONQUERORS IN THE 17th CENTURY*

AMERICA'S FIRST "FIRST LADY" Martha Washington *WAS NOT THE FIRST "FIRST LADY" OF THE U.S.* IT WAS JANE HANSON, THE WIFE OF JOHN HANSON OF MARYLAND, WHO WAS ELECTED PRESIDENT OF THE UNITED STATES IN CONGRESS ASSEMBLED IN 1781

ELIZABETH WIFE OF MAJOR GENERAL HAMILTON WHO WAS MARRIED FOR 47 YEARS AND NEVER DID **ONE** THING TO DISOBLIGE HER HUSBAND

Epitaph in Streatham, England

THE STRANGEST LEADERSHIP TEST IN HISTORY!

THE **CHIEF** OF THE NYASA TRIBE OF AFRICA, TO PROVE HIS FITNESS FOR OFFICE, WAS REQUIRED TO WAVE HIS SPEAR ABOVE HIS HEAD WHILE *BALANCING ON ONE LEG FROM SUNRISE TO SUNSET*

CLARENCE GREATHOUSE
(1843-1899)
of San Francisco, Calif.
THE U.S. CONSUL GENERAL IN YOKOHAMA, JAPAN, WAS APPOINTED PRIME MINISTER OF KOREA BY ITS KING, AND SERVED FOR YEARS

ZINC CRYSTALS OFTEN FORM THE SHAPE OF *A BEAUTIFUL FLOWER*

THE GRAVES OF THE SAMOYEDS OF SIBERIA ARE ALWAYS MARKED BY 2 SLEDS --PACKED WITH ALL THE EARTHLY POSSESSIONS OF THE DECEASED

THE **CHURCH OF ST. GEORGE** IN SALONIKA, GREECE, WAS CONSTRUCTED AS A PAGAN ROMAN TEMPLE -- WAS CONVERTED INTO A CHURCH BY EARLY CHRISTIANS --WAS MADE A MOSQUE WHEN TURKS CONQUERED THE CITY, AND IN THE 19th CENTURY AGAIN BECAME A CHURCH

A KEY USED AS A TALISMAN BY FARMERS OF SALZBURG, AUSTRIA, TO CURE STOMACH CRAMPS, IS MADE FROM THE SPINAL COLUMNS *OF SEVERAL SNAKES*

THE MAN WHO DEVOTED HIS ENTIRE LIFE TO A SINGLE PRAYER
GYULA VASZ (1871-1921) of Budapest, Hungary, RECITED THE LORD'S PRAYER 30 TIMES EACH DAY --HAVING LEARNED IT IN 150 LANGUAGES

THE MOTHERS WHO HAVE ARMS, LEGS--AND NERVES--OF STEEL!
NUNG WOMEN of Burma, CROSS THE ADUNG RIVER ON CABLES STRUNG 40 FEET ABOVE THE WATER, BALANCING ON A CANE RING AND PULLING THEMSELVES ACROSS THE 150-FOOT SPAN -- WITH AN INFANT STRAPPED TO THEIR BACKS

DOUGLAS McCURDY of Nova Scotia, WHO LATER BECAME LIEUT. GOVERNOR OF NOVA SCOTIA, MADE THE FIRST PLANE FLIGHT IN THE BRITISH EMPIRE --PILOTING THE SILVER DART OVER THE FROZEN BRAS D'OR LAKES IN BADDECK, N.S., ON FEB. 23, 1909

THE CHURCH OF WIENAU in Austria, WAS BUILT, IN 1877, BY 2 BROTHERS AS A MEANS OF RIDDING THEIR FARMS OF FIELD-STONES

MATERNITY ROCK, Locronan, France, A STONE ON WHICH CHILDLESS WOMEN SIT IN THE BELIEF IT WILL ASSURE THEM A SON OR DAUGHTER WITHIN A YEAR.

THE **BODY** of St. SHINJONI
IS REMOVED EACH YEAR FROM ITS COFFIN
IN THE MONASTERY THAT BEARS HIS
NAME IN ELBASAN, ALBANIA, AND
REWRAPPED IN A NEW WOOL COVERING --
*THE OLD WOOL BEING DISTRIBUTED IN
THE BELIEF IT CAN CURE THE INSANE*

A **CANARY**
OWNED BY A
MRS. GRABER
OF BERLIN,
GERMANY,
LEARNED TO SAY
" SING, SING,
MY SILLY
FOOL, SING "

THE SCAR THAT CREATED A NATIONAL FASHION!

KING FRANCIS I (1494-1547) OF FRANCE,
BECAME THE FIRST FRENCH MONARCH TO WEAR A BEARD, BECAUSE
HIS CHIN WAS SCARRED BY A BURNING TORCH TOSSED AT
HIM IN A GAME--- HIS DECISION MADE BEARDS FASHIONABLE

MEMORIAL TO A POTATO PATCH
A *BRONZE TABLET*
AT *VANCOUVER, WASH.,*
COMMEMORATING AN ATTEMPT
BY GENERAL U.S. GRANT AS
A YOUNG OFFICER TO
*GROW POTATOES FOR
THE OFFICERS' MESS AT
VANCOUVER BARRACKS*

SUBMITTED BY EMERY F. TOBIN
Vancouver, Wash.

3 MOUNTAIN PEAKS
ON THE BORDER BETWEEN
IRAN AND PAKISTAN ARE
EACH A DIFFERENT COLOR--
*ONE GREEN, THE SECOND PURPLE
AND THE THIRD BLUE*

MAY'S FOLLY

IN HADLOW, ENGLAND, A SPIRED HOME BUILT BY AN ECCENTRIC IN 1840 SO THE WIFE WHO LEFT HIM WOULD BE REMINDED OF HIM, BECAUSE IT WAS VISIBLE FROM ANY-WHERE IN THE AREA

MOSQUITO NETS

COVER THE GRAVES OF SOME NATIVES OF THE SAVAGE ISLANDS IN THE PACIFIC, IN THE BELIEF THAT IF THE DECEASED IS PLAGUED BY INSECTS *HE WILL LEAVE HIS TOMB*

THE DEAN OF ALL PITCHMEN

ANDREW SMITH OF LONDON, ENGLAND, WAS THE BARKER FOR A CARNIVAL CONCESSION *AT THE AGE OF 100*

THE VICTORY NUGGET

FOUND BY PETER PESINI, A LONE PROSPECTOR, IN MOONLIGHT CREEK IN THE PAPAROA RANGE OF AUSTRALIA AND *WEIGHING 87/4 OUNCES.* IT WAS SOLD IN 1917 FOR $1,750, BUT WOULD BE WORTH NEARLY $9,000 TODAY

THE GREAT ROCKING STONE

OF MERTOUTEK, *THE HOGAR REGION OF THE SAHARA DESERT*

ABIGAIL SMITH (1744-1818)

IN MARRYING PRESIDENT JOHN ADAMS, BECAME *ABIGAIL SMITH ADAMS.* THEIR DAUGHTER ABIGAIL ADAMS, BY MARRYING WILLIAM S. SMITH, *BECAME ABIGAIL ADAMS SMITH*

Submitted by Linda De Viney
Bolingbrook, Illinois

23

THE STRANGEST STRIPTEASE IN THE WORLD! MALE DANCERS, DURING THE FESTIVAL OF EGENGUN IN EDE, NIGERIA, WHIRL THROUGH A WILD DANCE IN A LONG ROBE --WHICH THEY MUST TURN INSIDE OUT WITHOUT EXPOSING THEIR BODIES

A MOHAMMEDAN MOSQUE WITH A MINARET 225 FEET HIGH, WAS CONSTRUCTED in Lednice, Czechoslovakia --WHICH NEVER HAD A MOHAMMEDAN RESIDENT. PRINCE ALOIS LICHTENSTEIN ORDERED THE MOSQUE BUILT AT A COST OF $400,000, IN 1797, TO PUNISH THE TOWN FOR ITS FAILURE TO PROVIDE HIM WITH A SUITABLE SITE FOR A CHURCH

ANNIE LOUISE CAREY AN AMERICAN OPERA STAR, HAD A VOICE RANGE OF 3½ OCTAVES --ENABLING HER TO SING ANY ROLE FROM SOPRANO TO HIGH BARITONE

PRISONER'S BRIDGE in Marrakesh, Morocco, WHICH HAS BEEN STANDING FOR 400 YEARS, WAS BUILT BY A FRENCH CAPTIVE AS THE PRICE FOR HIS FREEDOM

ROOSTER OWNED BY HENRY WAITT OF WAYNE, MAINE, THAT WAS FITTED WITH AN ARTIFICIAL LEG

WAGON WHEEL IN THE CITY HALL of Brno, Czechoslovakia, CONSTRUCTED BY A WHEELWRIGHT TO WIN A BET THAT HE COULD CHOP DOWN A TREE, CARRY IT HOME AND TURN IT INTO A WHEEL-- ALL IN ONE DAY

MARGARET THE DUCHESS OF DOUGLAS, Scotland, WHO DIED IN 1774, ALWAYS LEFT AS HER HOUSE GIFT TO A HOSTESS *THE GOWN SHE WORE*

2-STORY STONE HOUSES ARE BUILT BY THE 25,000 NATIVES OF HUNZA IN THE HIMALAYAS, *WHO OCCUPY ONLY THE GROUND FLOOR IN WINTER BECAUSE IT CAN BE HEATED EASIER, AND USE ONLY THE TOP FLOOR EACH SUMMER*

TACOMA ELEV. 7313 FT. POP. 17- MORE OR LESS — SIGN AT TACOMA, COLORADO

A **STATUE** OF A LEAPING LEOPARD THE HERALDIC EMBLEM OF NYASALAND, AFRICA, *DOUBLES AS A SUNDIAL*

THE **MAN** WHO COULD WRITE WITH HIS WRINKLES! GASPARD ABEILLE (1648-1718) CELEBRATED FRENCH POET AND PRIEST, IN HIS OLD AGE HAD SUCH AMAZING CONTROL OF THE WRINKLES ON HIS FACE *THAT HE COULD FORM THE LETTERS GA AND AB AT WILL ON EITHER CHEEK*

THE **WORLD'S LARGEST JACK-O'-LANTERN** CREATED ANNUALLY AT A REFINERY IN LOS ANGELES, CALIFORNIA, *HAS A MOUTH 73 FEET WIDE*

IDA SOPHIA SCUDDER
FOUNDER OF THE MISSIONARY MEDICAL COLLEGE FOR WOMEN IN VELLORE, INDIA, WAS SO POPULAR IN INDIA THAT LETTERS FROM AMERICA REACHED HER IN A LAND OF 350,000,000 PEOPLE ADDRESSED ONLY TO: *"DR. IDA, INDIA"*

THE **TEMPLE THAT HAS BEEN REBUILT 64 TIMES!**
THE SHRINE OF NAIKU at Ise, Japan, FIRST CONSTRUCTED IN THE YEAR 685, HAS BEEN DEMOLISHED AND THEN RESTORED *EVERY 20 YEARS*

A **SOLID GOLD COMB**
WAS STILL IN THE HAIR OF KING SOLOKHA OF THE SCYTHIANS WHEN HIS TOMB WAS DISCOVERED NEAR NIKOPOL, RUSSIA, *2,400 YEARS AFTER HIS BURIAL*

THE **MAN WHO RULED 2,000,000 PEOPLE WITH HIS FOOT!**
MOHAMMED I GHERAI (1480-1523) MONARCH OF THE CRIMEA, BECAUSE BOTH HIS HANDS BORE BATTLE WOUNDS WHEN HE ASCENDED HIS THRONE, SIGNED EVERY STATE DOCUMENT THROUGHOUT HIS REIGN BY STEPPING BAREFOOT INTO A DISH OF INK, *AND AFFIXING HIS FOOTPRINT AS HIS ROYAL SIGNATURE*

MY TRIP IS ENDED SEND MY SAMPLES HOME
Epitaph of THOMAS W. CAMPBELL A TRAVELING SALESMAN Aspen Grove Cemetery Burlington, Iowa

THE **MEMORIAL CHAPEL**
IN LINDAU, GERMANY, DEDICATED TO SOLDIERS SLAIN IN WORLD WAR I, ORIGINALLY HAD SERVED THE COMMUNITY AS A CHURCH FOR **900 YEARS**

THE CHUMBI VALLEY WATERFALL
NEAR PHARI, TIBET,
90 FEET HIGH,
*FREEZES SOLID FROM OCTOBER
UNTIL THE FOLLOWING SUMMER*

JACKIE MARMON
SEIZED BY MAORI HEADHUNTERS
WHEN HE AND 2 COMPANIONS WERE
SHIPWRECKED ON THE COAST OF
NEW ZEALAND IN 1800, WAS SPARED
BECAUSE HE WORE A HEAD
BANDAGE WHICH THE NATIVES
MISTOOK FOR THE EMBLEM OF A CHIEF

THE **PUBLIC WATER TROUGH**
ON HALLIG GRÖDE, IN THE NORTH FRISIAN ISLANDS,
IS A CONVERTED STONE COFFIN

HERE LIES THE BODY OF
ELIZABETH FARINGTON
WHO DEPARTED THIS LIFE
AUGUST 11, 1724, AGED 40,
AND 12 OF HER SONS AND DAUGHTERS,
ELIZABETH, HESTER, SARAH, ANN,
MARGARET, SARAH, JOSEPH, MARTHA,
THOMAS, ANNE, CHRISTINE AND MARY

TOMBSTONE EPITAPH IN IVER, ENGLAND

THE **CASTLE of POMPADOUR**
in France.
FROM WHICH THE NOTORIOUS MARQUISE
DE POMPADOUR TOOK HER TITLE,
WAS OWNED BY THE ROYAL
FAVORITE FOR 15 YEARS
-YET SHE NEVER SET FOOT IN
IT, BECAUSE OF A DREAM THAT SHE
WOULD DIE IF SHE ENTERED IT

THE **WOODEN BRIDGE** OVER THE RIVER KALI
GANDAKI, IN MUSTANG, IN THE HIMALAYAS,
WAS BUILT WITHOUT METAL OF ANY KIND
--*WOODEN PEGS, SUBSTITUTING FOR NAILS*

THE MOST AMAZING RESCUE IN THE HISTORY OF MOUNTAIN CLIMBING! ALMA WALTER A WAITRESS, WAS CLIMBING SWITZERLAND'S 12,840-FT. BERNINA PEAK, ROPED TO A GUIDE NAMED ZIPPERT, WHEN HE SUDDENLY LOST HIS FOOTING AND PLUNGED INTO A DEEP CREVICE. ZIPPERT SHOUTED TO THE GIRL TO CUT THE ROPE TO SAVE HERSELF, BUT SHE SUPPORTED HIS WEIGHT FOR AN HOUR UNTIL OTHER CLIMBERS ARRIVED --ALTHOUGH THE ROPE SHE HAD WOUND AROUND HER ARM CUT THROUGH TO THE BONE!

ANTONIO TALACCHINI (1767-1863) AN ITALIAN RAILROAD BUILDER, CONSTRUCTED HUNDREDS OF MILES OF RAILROADS AND DOZENS OF BRIDGES, STATIONS AND TUNNELS --YET HE NEVER ATTENDED SCHOOL AND COULD NEITHER READ NOR WRITE

THE PULPIT IN THE FACADE OF THE CATHEDRAL OF PERUGIA, ITALY, BUILT TO PERSUADE ST. BERNARDINO TO PREACH IN THAT CITY, TOOK 3 YEARS TO CONSTRUCT--AND WAS USED BY THE PATRON SAINT OF PERUGIA ONLY ONCE

THE CITY HALL OF GROSS ENZERSDORF, AUSTRIA, WAS CONSTRUCTED IN 1658 AS A CHURCH

THE GRAVE OF AN OVAHIMBA CHIEF IN AFRICA, IS DECORATED WITH THE SKULLS OF ALL THE CATTLE EATEN AT HIS FUNERAL

The BRIDE WHO MARRIED A SEVERED HEAD! PRINCE KHALID OF MULTAN, INDIA, SENT TO WAR ON HIS WEDDING DAY COMMITTED SUICIDE AFTER DIRECTING *THAT HIS HEAD BE CUT OFF AND SENT TO HIS FIANCÉE*

THE WEDDING WAS PERFORMED WITH THE GROOM'S HEAD ON A PILLOW

THE BRINE SHRIMP A CRUSTACEAN, HAS NOT CHANGED *IN 200,000,000 YEARS*

PAGODAS ON THE ISLAND OF BALI ARE BUILT WITH ELEVEN ROOFS --*SO ELEVEN GODS CAN BE OVERNIGHT GUESTS IN COMFORT AND PRIVACY*

HERE LIES A MAN THAT WAS KNOTT BORN
HIS FATHER WAS KNOTT BEFORE HIM
HE LIVED KNOTT AND DID KNOTT DIE
YET UNDERNEATH THIS STONE DOES LIE
KNOTT CHRISTENED, KNOTT BEGOT
AND HERE HE LIES AND YET WAS KNOTT.

Epitaph OF JOHN KNOTT, SHEFFIELD, ENGLAND

THE MAN WHO BLACKMAILED A KING! PIERRE-FRANÇOIS REAL (1751-1834) A RETIRED FRENCH ADMINISTRATOR IN FINANCIAL NEED, ANNOUNCED IN 1831 THAT HE WAS PUBLISHING HIS MEMOIRS --*AND RECEIVED $2,000,000 FOR THE MANUSCRIPT FROM KING LOUIS PHILIPPE OF FRANCE* THE MONARCH BURNED IT UPON DELIVERY

THE CHURCH OF ST. OUSTRILLE IN MONTOIRE, FRANCE, CLOSED IN 1789 BY THE FRENCH REVOLUTION *NOW SERVES AS AN APARTMENT HOUSE*

THE STRANGEST SUICIDE IN ALL HISTORY!

RAHMA IBN JABIR

A PIRATE OF KUWAIT IN THE PERSIAN GULF, WHO HAD 6 SHIPS AND 600 FOLLOWERS, VOWED THAT HE WOULD NOT DOFF HIS SHIRT UNTIL *IT WAS BLOWN FROM HIS BACK.* HE WORE THAT SHIRT FOR SEVERAL YEARS -- *UNTIL HE BLEW HIMSELF TO BITS BY SETTING FIRE TO A POWDER MAGAZINE*

JACOB
JACOB
JACOB
JACOB
(1830 - 1905),
A MANUFACTURER, LIVERPOOL, ENGLAND, NAMED FOR *OLDER BROTHERS WHO DIED IN INFANCY*

SACRED TO THE MEMORY OF JARED BATES HIS WIDOW AGED 24 WHO MOURNS AS ONE WHO CAN BE COMFORTED LIVES AT 7 ELM STREET THIS VILLAGE AND POSSESSES EVERY QUALIFICATION FOR A GOOD WIFE

Epitaph IN LINCOLN, MAINE

THE **GLASS EEL** of Australia IS SO TRANSPARENT THAT THE PAGES OF A BOOK CAN *BE READ THROUGH ITS BODY*

THE FOUNTAIN OF NEPTUNE IN LAEKEN, BELGIUM...

...BUILT FOR THE RESIDENCE OF KING LEOPOLD OF BELGIUM, IN 1903, IS A REPLICA OF A FOUNTAIN THE MONARCH ADMIRED IN BOLOGNA, ITALY --WHICH WAS DESIGNED BY A BELGIAN IN THE 16th CENTURY

THE **SQUABBLING COUPLE** JUGDULLUK, AFGHANISTAN. NATURAL STONE GATEWAY IN A MOUNTAIN PASS

THE STRANGEST SOLUTION TO A TRAFFIC BOTTLENECK IN ALL HISTORY

ERNEST WILSON, A BOSTON, MASS., BOTANIST, INJURED BY A ROCK SLIDE ON A NARROW MOUNTAIN LEDGE IN CHINA, ORDERED HIS LITTER PLACED CROSSWISE ON THE PATH WITH HIS FEET AT THE EDGE OF A 5,500-FOOT PRECIPICE—
AND ALLOWED A 40-MULE CARAVAN TO PASS OVER HIS SUPINE BODY   (1903)

ALEXANDER MACOMB
(1747-1832)
IN 1791 PURCHASED FROM THE STATE OF NEW YORK 3,934,899 ACRES OF LAND ON THE ST. LAWRENCE RIVER *FOR ONLY 16 CENTS AN ACRE.*
HE ACQUIRED AN AREA NEARLY TWICE THE SIZE OF DELAWARE AND RHODE ISLAND COMBINED FOR $629,583.84
—*BUT IT BANKRUPTED HIM*

THE TALL ORNAMENTS ON THE ROOF OF THE RI-BO-KANG TEMPLE, OF LHASA, TIBET, WERE CREATED BY TIGHTLY ROLLING *SUCCESSIVE SHEETS OF GOLD*

A **HUGE CARVED DRAGON** PRESERVED IN THE MUSEUM ON THE ISLAND OF RHODES, WAS CREATED BY THE GRAND MASTER OF RHODES IN THE 14th CENTURY TO PREPARE HIS HORSE FOR THE SIGHT OF THE LEGENDARY DRAGON HE LATER CLAIMED TO HAVE SLAIN

THE **BOOMERANG** IDENTIFIED WITH AUSTRALIAN ABORIGINES, WAS USED BY THE ANCIENT EGYPTIANS 3,000 YEARS AGO. ONE WAS FOUND DRAWN ON THE WALLS OF AN ANCIENT TEMPLE IN BADARI, EGYPT

HERE LIES THE BODY OF
JONATHAN TILTON
WHOSE FRIENDS REDUCED HIM
TO A SKELETON
THEY ROBBED HIM OUT OF ALL HE HAD
AND NOW REJOICE THAT HE IS DEAD

Epitaph of JONATHAN TILTON, CHILMARK, MASS.

THE **FATHER WHO REFUSED TO SACRIFICE A SERVANT'S CHILD TO SAVE HIS OWN!**
BYZANTINE EMPEROR MAURICE (539-602)
WAS SLAIN BY REBELS
ALONG WITH HIS WIFE AND 5 CHILDREN.
HIS YOUNGEST SON, JUSTINIAN, WAS STILL A BABY AND HIS NURSE OFFERED TO SUBSTITUTE HER OWN INFANT IN THE CRIB
--BUT THE EMPEROR REFUSED
TO PERMIT THE SWITCH

A **BIBLE**
3 FEET HIGH
AND CONSISTING
OF 7,596 PAGES,
CREATED BY
COLLECTING
EVERY BIBLE
LESSON PRINTED
IN THE AKRON,
OHIO, BEACON
JOURNAL
*OVER A
PERIOD OF
20 YEARS,
8 MONTHS
AND 18 DAYS*
Submitted by
Tilford E.
Lennon
Akron, Ohio

A **MEGASOMA GYAS INSECT**
GLUED TO A CARD
AND CONSIDERED DEAD,
SUDDENLY ON NOV. 2, 1949,
CAME TO LIFE AND
WALKED OFF THE CARD
London Entomological Soc.

A **BIRD REFUGE** near Stonewall, Manitoba,
HAS A 400-YARD POND
IN THE SHAPE OF A DUCK
Submitted by PAM DE WEESE, Long Beach,
New York

COL. JOSEPH FAY
(1752-1803)
OF BENNINGTON, VT.,
WAS ONE OF
5 BROTHERS,
ALL OF WHOM
FOUGHT IN
*THE BATTLE OF
BENNINGTON
IN 1777*

THE **CATHEDRAL OF SYRACUSE**
SICILY
WAS ORIGINALLY A PAGAN TEMPLE,
*AND IS THE OLDEST CHRISTIAN
CHURCH IN THE WEST*

THE MOST AMAZING FIRE-WALKING FEAT IN THE WORLD!

BLAZING FIRES ARE LIT IN EACH OF THE 101 BHIL VILLAGES OF INDIA EACH SPRING DURING THE FEAST OF HOLI, AND IN EVERY TOWN SOME 50 NATIVES WALK THROUGH THE FLAMES-- *BAREFOOTED AND WEARING FLIMSY GARMENTS!*

MORE THAN 5,000 ANNUALLY PERFORM THE FIRE WALK TO ASSURE SPEEDY RECOVERY OF A SICK RELATIVE --*YET NOT ONE PERSON HAS EVER SUFFERED BURNS*

DR. SAEED KHAN
A PHYSICIAN OF TEHERAN, IRAN, READ ALL THE WORKS OF SADI, HAFIZ AND JAMI, THE THREE GREATEST POETS OF ANCIENT PERSIA, *AT THE AGE OF 8*

THE LARVA
of the Buprestis Aurulenta insect, WHICH BORES INTO DOUGLAS FIRS IN CANADA, *EMERGES AS AN INSECT 24 YEARS LATER --OFTEN AFTER THE WOOD HAS BEEN USED IN BUILDINGS*

HERE LIES CUT DOWN LIKE UNRIPE FRUIT
THE WIFE OF DEACON AMOS SHUTE
SHE DIED OF DRINKING TOO MUCH COFFEE
ANNY DOMINY EIGHTEEN FORTY.

Epitaph in Canaan, N.H.

THE "REVOLVING" DOOR
OF THE GEORGE AND DRAGON INN, in Batheaston, England, IS A 1,000-GALLON WINE BARREL

THE CHILDREN'S CHURCH
THE CHURCH OF SEIFFEN, Germany, *WAS CONSTRUCTED AS A COPY OF A TOY CHURCH MADE HERE FOR CHILDREN IN EVERY PART OF THE WORLD*

A MINIATURE SILVER TOWER HELD BY A STATUE OF THE APOSTLE JAMES IN THE CATHEDRAL OF SANTIAGO de COMPOSTELA IN SPAIN, CONTAINS ONE OF THE APOSTLE'S TEETH

LOADED DONKEYS WANDER ALONE THROUGH MERIDA, SPAIN, TRUSTED BY THEIR OWNERS TO VISIT DISTANT WELLS *AND THEN FIND THEIR WAY BACK*

"SILBO GOMERO" USED BY NATIVES OF THE ISLAND OF GOMERA IN THE CANARY ISLANDS AS A MEANS OF COMMUNICATIONS FOR CENTURIES, *IS A LANGUAGE OF WHISTLES*

THE **SANCTUARY OF SAN FRANCESCO** IN LULA, ITALY, WAS BUILT IN 1770 BY FRANCESCO TOLA, A HIGHWAYMAN, TO FULFILL A VOW THAT *HE WOULD CONSTRUCT IT IF FOUND INNOCENT AT HIS TRIAL FOR ROBBERY AND MURDER*

THE **CLOCK** IN THE ROOM IN WHICH SIMON BOLIVAR DIED IN SANTA MARTA, COLOMBIA, ON DEC. 17, 1830, *HAS BEEN STOPPED FOR 143 YEARS AT THE EXACT INSTANT HE PASSED AWAY*

THE 2 MINARETS OF THE MOSQUE OF AURANGZEB IN BENARES, INDIA, EACH 147 FEET HIGH *BOTH LEAN 15 INCHES OFF CENTER*

THE **GARDEN** OF MARCUS LUCRETIUS, IN POMPEII, ITALY, DESTROYED IN THE YEAR 79, HAS BEEN RESTORED WITH THE SAME TYPE FLOWERS PLANTED EXACTLY WHERE THEY WERE BY LOCATING AND IDENTIFYING *ROOTS THAT FLOURISHED 1,895 YEARS AGO*

THE **LITTLE PREACHER** **ALBRECHT von HALLER** (1708-1777) THE SWISS BOTANIST, PHYSIOLOGIST, BIBLIOGRAPHER, POET, NOVELIST AND ANATOMIST, MASTERED LATIN AND GREEK AND WROTE A CHALDEAN GRAMMAR AND A HEBREW AND GREEK DICTIONARY WHEN HE WAS ONLY 9, *AND DELIVERED A SERMON AT THE AGE OF 4*

THE **OLDEST BOW** THE HOLMEGAARD BOW FOUND IN HOLMEGAARD, DENMARK, WAS MADE OF ELMWOOD 10,000 YEARS AGO

ELIZA JANE NICHOLSON (1849-1896) *WAS AMERICA'S FIRST WOMAN PUBLISHER OF A DAILY NEWSPAPER* SHE WAS PUBLISHER OF THE NEW ORLEANS PICAYUNE FROM 1876 TO 1896

THE **NEST** OF THE REED WARBLER IS MADE BY WEAVING LONG GRASS AROUND HALF A DOZEN TALL REEDS

THE **DOOR** OF ST. NICHOLAS CHURCH, IN STEINBÜHL, GERMANY, IS COVERED WITH HORSESHOES, *TO ASSURE GOOD HEALTH FOR THE ANIMALS THAT WORE THEM*

THE PROPHECY THAT HUNG BY A THREAD!

A STATUE OF THE MADONNA, ATOP ALBERT CATHEDRAL, IN FRANCE, DISLODGED BY A GERMAN BOMBARDMENT IN 1915, DANGLED PRECARIOUSLY FROM ITS THIN SUPPORT FOR 3 YEARS.

FRENCHMEN REPEATEDLY INSISTED THE WAR WOULD END WHEN THE STATUE FINALLY FELL --GERMAN SHELLS FINALLY HURLED THE STATUE TO THE GROUND ON NOV.10 1918 -- AND THE ARMISTICE WAS SIGNED THE NEXT DAY

A KITE
BUILT AND FLOWN BY WALTER BORESEN AND EDWARD BAKER, BOTH OF WEST HAVEN, CONN., *MEASURED 9' 8" 10' 8"*

THE CLIMBER
NEAR LUISENTHAL, IN THE THURINGIAN FOREST, GERMANY, NATURAL STONE FORMATION

THE TAMBOURINE DOVE
of WEST AFRICA, HAS A CRY THAT SOUNDS *LIKE THUMPING A TAMBOURINE*

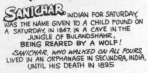

SANICHAR INDIAN FOR SATURDAY, WAS THE NAME GIVEN TO A CHILD FOUND ON A SATURDAY, IN 1867, IN A CAVE IN THE JUNGLE OF BULANDSHAHR, BEING REARED BY A WOLF!
SANICHAR, WHO WALKED ON ALL FOURS, LIVED IN AN ORPHANAGE IN SECUNDRA, INDIA, UNTIL HIS DEATH IN 1895

LIEUT. JOHN J. DEVLIN
WAS ON ACTIVE DUTY IN THE ELMIRA, N.Y., POLICE DEPT. FOR **64 YEARS** -- RETIRING AT THE AGE OF **89**

THE POET WHO FOUND THAT CRITICS ARE TYRANTS WITH SHORT MEMORIES!

DARA CHEKOUR (1616-1643)
SON OF THE MOGUL EMPEROR SHAH JEHAN,
BUILDER OF THE TAJ MAHAL, TWICE SAVED
DSIHAN KHAN, RULER OF TATTA, FROM DEATH.
YET DSIHAN IN 1643 BETRAYED DARA TO
ENEMIES TO BE STRANGLED--*BECAUSE
HE FELT DARA WROTE BAD POETRY !*

THE AQUEDUCT OF ARCUEIL
France, 261 FEET LONG,
WAS BUILT IN SUCCESSIVE STAGES
BY ROMAN EMPEROR JULIAN,
QUEEN MARIE de MEDICI
OF FRANCE, AND NAPOLEON III,
OVER A PERIOD OF 1,520 YEARS

THE **HUNCHBACKED SALMON** REACH THE
KAMCHATKA RIVER IN SIBERIA FROM THE
SEA, BUT THE STRENUOUS ASCENT OF THE
RIVER ALWAYS CAUSES THEIR UNIQUE
CURVATURE OF THE SPINE

THE FIRST IRON BATTLESHIP
H.M.S. WARRIOR,
CONSTRUCTED BY THE BRITISH IN 1860,
BECAME THE FIRST IRON WARSHIP
--*BECAUSE IT WAS FOUND WOOD COULD NOT
SUPPORT ITS HEAVY GUNS AND
STEAM ENGINES*

ELSBET von CELLINKON
(1244-1335)
WHO ENTERED THE CONVENT
OF TÖSS IN SWITZERLAND,
AT THE AGE OF 6,
*WAS A NUN
FOR 86 YEARS*

LEON ALLATIUS
(1586-1669) AN ITALIAN AUTHOR
USED THE SAME QUILL PEN
FOR **40** YEARS
--AND WHEN HE LOST IT
DIED OF GRIEF

ALAGAS SOUCHEK
WAS A SHEPHERD
IN THE RUSSIAN UKRAINE
FOR THE SAME FAMILY
FOR 84 YEARS--
HE WORKED UNTIL HIS
DEATH AT THE AGE
OF 104

The **SNAIL THAT WEARS A HAT**
THE KEEL SNAIL of the Mediterranean
IS TOPPED BY A TRANSPARENT SHELL
SHAPED LIKE A HAT--
IT SWIMS ON ITS BACK, USING ITS
SINGLE FIN AS A STEERING OAR

The **GREAT GATE of SUNG CHUNG YO**
China
WAS CARVED ENTIRELY FROM A
SINGLE BLOCK OF MARBLE--
IT WAS COMPLETED IN 14 YEARS
BY ONE MAN WORKING ALONE

The **CASTLE of La BARGE**
near THIERS, FRANCE,
HAS BEEN INHABITED BY THE SAME FAMILY
MORE THAN 400 YEARS

THE CABLE CARS of San Francisco, Calif. ARE THE ONLY OFFICIAL NATIONAL MONUMENT *THAT MOVES*

THE MOST AMAZING MARITAL RECORD IN ALL HISTORY
JEAN MEURAT-FEUILLE (1781-1901) WHO LIVED IN 3 CENTURIES, CELEBRATED 2 GOLDEN WEDDING ANNIVERSARIES -- WITH 2 SUCCESSIVE WIVES (Aveyron, France)

KINSLEY S. BINGHAM
(1808-1861)
BECAME THE 11th GOVERNOR OF MICHIGAN IN 1854 AS THE REPUBLICAN PARTY CAME INTO BEING IN THE U.S. --*THE FIRST G.O.P. GOVERNOR IN THE NATION*

THE TOWER OF THE KORNHÄUSEL IN Vienna, Austria, BUILT AS A STUDIO BY ARCHITECT JOSEPH KORNHÄUSEL, WAS MADE ACCESSIBLE ONLY BY A DRAWBRIDGE TO *DISCOURAGE INTERRUPTIONS BY HIS WIFE*

THE FIRST STETHOSCOPE
WAS INVENTED BY DR. THEOPHILE LAENNEC (1781-1826) *WHO PATTERNED IT AFTER A ROLLED UP SHEET OF PAPER WHICH HE HAD USED TO EXAMINE FEMININE PATIENTS*

CALVARY STAIRWAY
IN POLLENSA, ON THE ISLAND OF MAJORCA
HAS **365** STEPS
-- *ONE FOR EACH DAY OF THE YEAR*

THE **ONE-LEGGED ALPINIST**
G.W. YOUNG
ONE YEAR AFTER HE LOST A LEG IN
WORLD WAR I, RESUMED HIS HOBBY
OF MOUNTAIN CLIMBING IN SWITZERLAND
-- *CONQUERING MT. GREPON, 11,700' HIGH;
MT. ZINAL, 13,849'; THE MATTERHORN,
14,690' AND MT. ROSA, 15,203'*

THE **GRAVE** OF
CHIEF KINTAHOOK,
OF THE CAPE FOX
INDIANS-- *WHO
WAS A MEMBER
OF THE BEAR CLAN--*
IN THE INDIAN
CEMETERY ON
PENNOCK ISLAND,
ALASKA,
*IS GUARDED BY
2 CONCRETE
BEARS*
Submitted by
EMERY F. TOBIN
Vancouver, Wash.

SENECA
THE ROMAN STATESMAN
AND PHILOSOPHER,
OWNED **500** TABLES MADE
OF CITRUS WOOD,
EACH VALUED AT
1,000,000 SESTERCES
--*THE TOTAL EQUIVALENT OF
$20,000,000*

THE "CUMBERLAND"
A 3-DECK BATTLESHIP WITH 80 GUNS
STARTED SERVICE IN THE BRITISH FLEET,
WAS CAPTURED IN 1707 AND SERVED THE
FRENCH FOR 5 YEARS, WAS SOLD TO SPAIN
--AND IN 1718 WAS
RECAPTURED BY THE BRITISH

THE BRIDES WHO BECOME MORE VALUABLE EACH TIME THEY MARRY
A WOMAN
OF THE TURKOMAN TRIBE, in Iran,
COSTS THE GROOM THE EQUIVALENT
OF $79 IN HER FIRST MARRIAGE AND
THE FIGURE INCREASES BY THAT
AMOUNT EACH TIME SHE WEDS
--A WOMAN MARRYING FOR THE 10th
TIME BEING VALUED AT $790 --
*THE HIGHER VALUE IS THE RESULT
OF THE EXPERIENCE SHE HAS GAINED
--IN RUG WEAVING AND HOUSEKEEPING*

THE BRICK WALLS
IN THE VILLAGE OF SIALIK, IRAN, ARE MADE
OF MUD KNEADED BY HAND 6,000 YEARS AGO
--*THE OLDEST BRICKS IN THE WORLD*

THE TWO-WAY RIVER
THE KARAS RIVER
NORMALLY FLOWS FROM
RUMANIA TO YUGOSLAVIA AND
INTO THE DANUBE--BUT WHEN
THE DANUBE RIVER FLOODS, THE
KARAS FLOWS FROM YUGOSLAVIA
TO RUMANIA AND EMPTIES
INTO THE TEMES RIVER

THE FLANNEL MULLEIN
REQUIRES 2 YEARS TO COME INTO
FULL BLOOM-- PRODUCING A
ROSETTE OF BASIL LEAVES THE
FIRST YEAR AND ADDING A TALL
FLOWERING STEM THE NEXT

THE CONVICT WHO IN 22 YEARS NEVER HAD AN IDLE HOUR!
KARL HANS
WEISSKOPF
CONFINED TO A CELL IN
THE PENITENTIARY OF
EBRACH, BAVARIA FROM
1927 TO 1949 FOR MURDER,
MASTERED 9 LANGUAGES
IN PRISON, INCLUDING
SANSKRIT, LATIN AND
GREEK--AND MEMORIZED
*THE ENTIRE GERMAN
ENCYCLOPEDIA OF
12 VOLUMES*

THE CHURCH of BOURBOURG in France, WAS UNDER CONSTRUCTION FOR 352 YEARS

THE STRANGEST VICTORY MARCH IN HISTORY!
CALIPH OMAR RULER OF THE ARAB WORLD IN 637, TO ACCEPT THE SURRENDER OF THE CITY OF JERUSALEM FROM THE GREEKS, JOURNEYED 900 MILES ACROSS THE DESERT FROM MECCA--ACCOMPANIED ONLY BY A SINGLE SERVANT WITH WHOM HE ALTERNATED LEADING AND RIDING THEIR LONE CAMEL.

WHEN THEY REACHED JERUSALEM, IT WAS THE SERVANT'S TURN TO RIDE AND THE CALIPH WAS LEADING THE CAMEL

THE CLAY NEST of the TARANTULA TO PROTECT IT FROM ENEMIES, HAS A TRAP DOOR COMPRISING 30 LAYERS OF SILK AND DIRT WHICH CAN SHUT OUT EVEN WATER AND AIR

THOMAS L. HAMER
(1800-1846)
ENLISTED IN THE U.S. ARMY IN THE MEXICAN WAR AS A PRIVATE AND WAS PROMOTED TO BRIGADIER GENERAL THE NEXT DAY
July 1, 1846

THE BARN
of MAURICE W. WARNER near Churchville, N.Y., HAS 68 STALLS IN WHICH HE HAS INSTALLED RED CARPETING

GREAT SALT LAKE, in Larnaca, Cyprus, DRIES OUT COMPLETELY EACH SUMMER *PROVIDING NATIVES WITH A CONVENIENT SUPPLY OF SALT*

THE VIENNESE PROGRESSION
EMIL RADEGUNT (1801-1871)
of Vienna, Austria, MARRIED 4 WOMEN
THE FIRST, MARIANNE, GAVE HIM
TWINS
THE SECOND, KONSTANZE, BORE
TRIPLETS
THE THIRD, THERESIA, HAD
QUADRUPLETS
THE FOURTH, ANNA, BORE
QUINTUPLETS

POTATO DUCK

GROWN BY
RALPH ARUNDALE
Sandoval, N.M.
Submitted by
Mrs. CLEO HUGHES
Albuquerque, N.M.

A **CHRISTMAS CACTUS**
IN THE HOME OF
MRS. JAMES WARRICK,
of Royalton, Minn.,
*HAS BLOOMED
ANNUALLY
FOR 52
YEARS*

WILLIAM CAREY
(1761-1834)
TRANSLATED
THE BIBLE INTO
*26 HINDU
LANGUAGES
AND DIALECTS*

A **NICKEL** NOTCHED BY PATRICK CRONIN TO TEST THE SHARPNESS OF A NEW KNIFE *WAS RETURNED TO HIM IN CHANGE FOR A PURCHASE WEEKS AFTER HE HAD SPENT IT* (Wilmington, Del.)

THE CHURCH THAT WAS FOUND BY A DREAM THE CHURCH OF STAVROS NOW USED FOR REGULAR SERVICES ON THE ISLAND OF PERISSA, GREECE, HAD BEEN BURIED FOR 400 YEARS UNTIL A FARMER NAMED GERASSIMOS, IN THE VILLAGE OF GONIA, GREECE, SAW THE LOCATION OF THE LOST EDIFICE *IN A DREAM!*

FEMALE ATTACUS MOTHS HAVE HUGE WINGS WHICH THEY VIBRATE TO *SEND MESSAGES*

THE MOST SHIFTY-EYED MAN IN ALL HISTORY *SULTAN MULEY ZEIDAN* RULER OF MOROCCO FROM 1603 TO 1630 HAD A BLUE RIGHT EYE AND A BLACK LEFT EYE *--BUT THE COLORS SHIFTED WHENEVER HE BECAME ANGRY*

MARRIED MEN OF MARLING, IN SOUTH TYROL, PROCLAIM THEIR MARITAL STATUS *BY WEARING BLACK HATS* BACHELORS IN THE COMMUNITY WEAR GREEN HEADGEAR

THIS IS THE EPITAPH OF THE DEAN OF ST. ASAPH WHO BY KEEPING A TABLE BETTER THAN HE WAS ABLE RAN MUCH INTO DEBT WHICH IS NOT PAID YET

EPITAPH of DEAN LLOYD IN THE CEMETERY OF RUTHIN, WALES

THE MAN WHO LIVED UP TO HIS NAME!

MARTINUS KALKOEN (1804-1901) OF AMSTERDAM, WHOSE SURNAME IN DUTCH MEANS "TURKEY," ATE TURKEY FOR LUNCH AND DINNER *EVERY DAY FOR 43 YEARS*

THE FIRST LORD PALMERSTON (1673-1757)
WAS GIVEN A LIFETIME APPOINTMENT AS TAX COLLECTOR OF IRELAND *WHEN HE WAS 7 YEARS OF AGE*

A CIRCULAR HOUSE
at Arzachena, Sardinia,
BUILT IN A HOLLOW BOULDER

EUROPE'S FIRST SKYSCRAPER

THE WHITE HOUSE BUILT IN ROTTERDAM, NETHERLANDS, IN 1897, AN OFFICE BUILDING 151 FEET HIGH, WAS THE FIRST STRUCTURE IN EUROPE EQUIPPED WITH AN ELEVATOR. IT WAS SO STURDY THAT IT ESCAPED UNHARMED ALTHOUGH GERMAN BOMBS IN WORLD WAR II RAZED THE REST OF ROTTERDAM

HOUSE OF WORDS
THE VILLA OF MEDAN near Paris, France,
WAS JUST A FARMHOUSE WHEN IT WAS PURCHASED
BY EMILE ZOLA, BUT HE ADDED EITHER
ANOTHER TOWER OR ANOTHER ANNEX
*WITH THE PROCEEDS OF EACH
OF 10 SUCCESSFUL NOVELS*

THE
**GREATEST
LINGUIST
IN ALL HISTORY!**
HANS KONON BARON
Von der GABELENZ
(1807-1874)
of Altenburg, Germany,
MERELY BY READING
*TAUGHT HIMSELF
208 LANGUAGES*

A HOLLOW STONE
CONSIDERED BY THE USSUKUMA TRIBE (Africa)
AN INFALLIBLE RAINMAKER
HERBS WERE GROUND IN THE STONE'S
OPENING BY THE TRIBE'S MAGICIAN

THE
**MATRIMONIAL
SHRINE OF
CEROUX-
MOUSTY**
Belgium

*YOUNG
GIRLS*
LONG-
BELIEVED
THAT IF
THEY HUNG
A SHOE
OUTSIDE
THE SHRINE
*THEY
WOULD
BE
MARRIED
WITHIN
THE
YEAR*

THE **HUMAN STAMP OF DIVINE CLEMENCY!**
KING DJAHWAR ben MOHAMMED
MOORISH RULER OF CORDOBA, SPAIN, (1031-1043)
NEVER SIGNED A DEATH WARRANT DURING
HIS ENTIRE REIGN BECAUSE HE CONSIDERED
THE BIRTH MARK ON HIS FOREHEAD
--" LA" THE ARABIC WORD FOR "NO"--
A *DIVINE OBJECTION TO ANY DEATH SENTENCE*
WHEN AN OFFICIAL PROTESTED HIS DECISION
THE KING'S WRATH MADE THE "LA"
STAND OUT LIKE FIERY LETTERS

A **DAGGER** MADE IN GERMANY IN 1580
DOUBLED AS A *WHEEL LOCK PISTOL*

WILLIAM CORBETT OF RENTON, WASHINGTON, BY KARATE CHOPS WITH HIS BARE HANDS IN A PERIOD OF 17 HOURS, *SHATTERED 5,000 BRICKS*

THE **WASHERWOMEN'S CUDGEL** near Chengte, China, NATURAL STONE FORMATION, NAMED FOR THE FACT THAT ITS SHAPE RESEMBLES THE CLUB USED BY CHINESE WOMEN TO POUND THEIR LAUNDRY

THE TOWER OF KYBURG CASTLE IN SWITZERLAND, HAS WALLS **23** FEET THICK

THE **CHURCH** of the **HOLY TRINITY** in York, England, CONSTRUCTED IN 1236, IS OPENED FOR SERVICES *ONLY ONCE EACH YEAR*

THE FUNERAL IN WHICH 60 QUEENS MARCHED TO THEIR DEATH!

THE **60** WIDOWS OF MAHARAJAH MAN SINGH, OF AMBER, INDIA, AFTER HE WAS SLAIN IN BATTLE IN 1615 FORMED A LINE IN FRONT OF HIS FUNERAL PYRE AND ONE AFTER THE OTHER THREW THEMSELVES UPON IT --*TO BE BURNED ALIVE!*

FRIEDRICH NIETZSCHE
(1844-1900)

THE GERMAN PHILOSOPHER AS A SCHOOLBOY OF 9 IN NAUMBURG--TO EMULATE A FEAT OF COURAGE BY THE ANCIENT ROMAN MUCIUS SCAEVOLA-- *IGNITED HALF A DOZEN MATCHES IN THE PALM OF HIS BARE HAND AND ENDURED THE PAIN OF HAVING THEM BURN TO ASH WITHOUT TWITCHING A SINGLE MUSCLE*

THE LARGEST MOUNTAIN CROSS IN THE WORLD

THE MEMORIAL CROSS, ERECTED IN 1950 ATOP MOUNT TRAUNSTEIN, AUSTRIA, TO HONOR THE DEAD OF BOTH WORLD WARS WEIGHS 8,000 POUNDS AND THE STEEL, CEMENT AND SAND USED IN ITS CONSTRUCTION WERE CARRIED TO THE PEAK BY 800 PERSONS --200 OF THEM WOMEN

THE CALIFORNIA QUAIL

SEEMS TO BE REPEATING CONSTANTLY, "WHERE ARE YOU?" AND, "SIT RIGHT DOWN!"

THE CHAPEL OF HOHFLUHE

IN SWITZERLAND, WAS BUILT IN 1250 BY AGNES de MANGEPAN IN GRATITUDE FOR THE SAFE RETURN OF HER INFANT SON, MARKARD, WHO HAD BEEN *CARRIED OFF BY AN EAGLE-* THE BIRD DEPOSITED THE BABY SAFELY ON THE BANK OF A NEARBY RIVER

THE FIRST RAINCHECK

- A MARKER ISSUED TO A VISITOR TO A ROMAN CIRCUS 1800 YEARS AGO IT WAS DUG UP NEAR Walthamstow, England

THE WOMAN WHO WAS DEPRIVED OF A THRONE
BY A BOLT OF *LIGHTNING*!

THE MARQUISE d'ENTRAIGUES (1579-1633)
WAS GIVEN $100,000 AND A SIGNED CONTRACT OF
MARRIAGE BY KING HENRY IV of France.
BUT ON THE DAY SET FOR HER WEDDING
*LIGHTNING STRUCK HER BEDROOM
AND LEFT HER SO SHAKEN THAT
SHE NEVER BECAME QUEEN OF FRANCE*

A **ROSARY**
FOUND IN AN
ANCIENT TEMPLE
IN CENTRAL ASIA
BY SVEN HEDIN, THE
SWEDISH EXPLORER,
HAD BEEN MADE BY
*STRINGING HUMAN BONES
ON TAMARISK GRASS*

TATU
A BRAZILIAN
FISHERMAN AND
2 COMPANIONS
--ALL OVER 60
YEARS OF AGE--
SAILED THE
ATLANTIC FROM
FORTALEZO IN
NORTHERN BRAZIL,
TO RIO GRANDE
AND BACK--
A DISTANCE OF
7,500 MILES--
*ON AN OPEN
RAFT MADE OF
6 CEDAR BEAMS*
(1951)

THE **BAUHINIA PLANT**
IN THE KALAHARI DESERT OF AFRICA
PRODUCES FLOWERS THAT LAST ONLY ONE DAY, BUT
IT GROWS NEW BLOOMS DAILY FOR MONTHS

49

THE STRANGEST ROMANCE IN HISTORY

SERGEANT WILLIAM POPPLE,
A BRITISH SOLDIER ON HIS WAY TO
INDIA, SHOPPING IN A STATIONERY
STORE IN DUBLIN IN 1870
SEIZED A SALESWOMAN'S CUFFLINK AND FLED --
5 YEARS LATER POPPLE, UNABLE TO RECALL
THE STORE, VISITED EVERY STATIONERY
SHOP IN DUBLIN UNTIL THE CUFFLINK WAS
RECOGNIZED BY A SALESWOMAN
*--WHOM SERGEANT POPPLE PROMPTLY
PROPOSED TO AND MARRIED !*

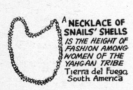

A **NECKLACE OF
SNAILS' SHELLS**
*IS THE HEIGHT OF
FASHION AMONG
WOMEN OF THE
YAHGAN TRIBE*
Tierra del Fuego,
South America

MEDICINAL TEA LEAVES
PRESSED INTO THE SHAPE OF
ANIMALS, BIRDS AND REPTILES,
WERE USED BY NATIVES OF
MANAOS, BRAZIL, FOR CENTURIES
AS MONEY

THE MOST HOSPITABLE HOTEL

THE MONASTERY OF TROYAN, in Bulgaria,
FOR SEVERAL CENTURIES WAS A SUMMER
HOTEL IN WHICH ALL TRAVELERS WERE
GIVEN 3 DAYS OF FOOD AND LODGING
WITHOUT CHARGE-
GUESTS PAID ONLY FOR THE TIME THEY STAYED
IN THE HOTEL AFTER THE INITIAL 3 DAYS

COL. JAMES SKINNER
(1778-1841) of Delhi, India,
TO TRIPLE HIS CHANCES OF
RECOVERY FROM BATTLE WOUNDS
VOWED THAT IF RESTORED TO
HEALTH HE WOULD BUILD
*A CHURCH, A MOSQUE
AND A HINDU TEMPLE-*
HE REGAINED HIS STRENGTH
AND THE 3 EDIFICES HE
BUILT STILL STAND IN DELHI

**THE CEDAR OF
LEBANON TREE**
ATTAINS MATURITY
ONLY AFTER
500 YEARS

THE PARADISE FISH
of North China,
IN SELECTING HIS MATE
*KILLS EVERY PROSPECTIVE
BRIDE HE FINDS
UNACCEPTABLE*

AGENOR PAILLET. (1860-1915) OF PARIS, FRANCE, WAS THE FATHER OF 4 CHILDREN WHO WERE BORN ON DECEMBER 12th, MARCH 11th, SEPTEMBER 4th and JANUARY 4th -- --AND BY HIS NAMESAKE SON, AGENOR PAILLET Jr., BECAME THE GRANDFATHER OF 4 CHILDREN WHO WERE BORN ON DECEMBER 12th, MARCH 11th, SEPTEMBER 4th and JANUARY 4th

THE **HOLY MAN** OF THE KOLI TRIBE, IN SAKERWADI, INDIA, PROTECTS HIS COMMUNITY AGAINST DISEASE BY CIRCLING IT ONCE EACH YEAR BALANCING ON HIS HEAD *A POT OF BURNING COAL*

A **MINIATURE CHURCH** BUILT IN HANOVER, GERMANY, IN 1966, WITH **40,000 MATCHES**

COCONUT PALMS SERVED IN TAHITI FOR CENTURIES *AS SUN DIALS* THE NATIVES KNEW IT WAS NOON WHEN A TREE WAS CIRCLED BY ITS SHADOW

ABNORMALLY **CURVED BOAR TUSKS** ARE USED BY NATIVES OF THE NEW BRITAIN ISLANDS AS AMULETS BECAUSE THEY ARE SO RARE THEY ARE *CONSIDERED A SACRED PROTECTION*

THE TULE PERCH of California, IS THE ONLY SWEETWATER FISH *OF THE 17 SPECIES OF ITS FAMILY*

THE MARINER WHO WAS SAVED FROM DROWNING --BY THE SEA! CAPTAIN BRISCO, MASTER OF THE "GRACE HARWAR," WASHED OVERBOARD BY A GIGANTIC WAVE EN ROUTE FROM DELAGOA BAY, E.AFRICA, TO GISBORNE, N.Z., WAS SAVED FROM CERTAIN DEATH WHEN A SECOND WAVE FLUNG HIM BACK TO HIS ORIGINAL POSITION ON THE SHIP'S BRIDGE
THE VESSEL WAS DISABLED BUT WAS RIGHTED A WEEK LATER AND TOWED TO SAFETY (Dec.25,1900)

A PAPUAN NATIVE WHEN HE GOES COURTING, CAN ONLY MUMBLE BECAUSE HE WEARS SUSPENDED BY A HOOK FROM HIS NOSE A LARGE MOUTH PLUG

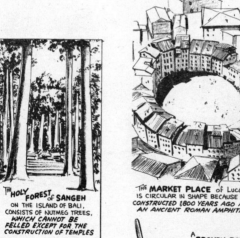

THE HOLY FOREST OF SANGEH ON THE ISLAND OF BALI, CONSISTS OF NUTMEG TREES, WHICH CANNOT BE FELLED EXCEPT FOR THE CONSTRUCTION OF TEMPLES

THE MARKET PLACE of Lucca, Italy, IS CIRCULAR IN SHAPE BECAUSE IT WAS CONSTRUCTED 1800 YEARS AGO AROUND AN ANCIENT ROMAN AMPHITHEATRE

A BROKEN POT and PESTLE USED BY A WOMAN OF THE IBA-WE TRIBE OF GWEMBE, AFRICA, BECOMES HER GRAVESTONE

A RESTAURANT
IN THE CHASM OF PADIRAC, FRANCE,
IS LOCATED 289 FEET UNDERGROUND

THE TOMBSTONE
OF GUIDARELLO GUIDARELLI,
WHO DIED IN 1501 IN A
FIGHT FOR POSSESSION OF
A WOMAN'S SCARF, IS VISITED
EACH YEAR BY THOUSANDS
OF ROMANTIC GIRLS WHO
BELIEVE THAT KISSING
HIS MARBLE IMAGE
WILL ASSURE THEM
HAPPINESS IN LOVE

TOBACCO
WAS GIVEN THAT NAME BY
GONZALEZ OVIEDO, FIRST
CHRONICLER OF THE NEW WORLD,
AS A RESULT OF A
MISUNDERSTANDING.
CARIBBEAN NATIVES CALLED THEIR
Y-SHAPED PIPES TOBACCOS
--AND WHEN OVIEDO ASKED ONE
WHAT HE WAS SMOKING, IN 1535,
THE NATIVE THOUGHT HE WAS
REFERRING TO THE PIPE

THE
**STONE
BASE**
OF A
PILLAR
IN THE
CATHEDRAL
OF
SANTIAGO DE
COMPOSTELA
-- THE
HOLIEST
SANCTUARY
IN SPAIN--
SERVED IN
ANCIENT
TIMES AS
A PAGAN
ALTAR TO
JUPITER

**THE MAN WHO
STRANGLED A TIGER
WITH HIS BARE HANDS**
SIR EDWARD WINTER (1622-1686) of Battersea,
England, ATTACKED BY A HUGE TIGER WHILE HE
WAS UNARMED ON A CAMPING TRIP IN INDIA,
CHOKED IT TO DEATH WITH HIS HANDS!

DOUGHNUT TOMATO
A TOMATO,
15 INCHES IN CIRCUMFERENCE,
WITH A HOLE IN ITS CENTER
Grown by E.C.Knott, Summerland, B.C.

A **POLAR BEAR** PROVIDED NEEDED MEAT FOR A DUTCH ARCTIC EXPEDITION IN NOVA ZEMBLA IN 1596 WHEN IT WAS SHOT BY THE EXPLORERS *AS IT WAS PEERING INTO THE EXPEDITION'S BEEF BARREL*

THE **CHURCH OF ST. LEONHARD** in Tölz, Germany, IS GIRDLED BY A CHAIN BECAUSE ST. LEONHARD, IN THE 5TH CENTURY, WAS EMPOWERED BY A FRENCH KING TO FREE ANY PRISONER --AND ALWAYS WORE THE CHAINS OF A PRISONER HE HAD RELEASED

A **TRIPLE BEER MUG** CREATED IN GERMANY *FOR TRULY GREGARIOUS IMBIBERS*

THE **ASTOUNDING COINCIDENCE THAT CURED A 9-YEAR CASE OF AMNESIA!** JEAN CASTEL, A 15-YEAR-OLD FRENCH YOUTH, INJURED WHILE FLEEING FROM GERMAN SOLDIERS IN 1915 *SUFFERED TOTAL AMNESIA* 9 YEARS LATER HE MET AND FELL IN LOVE WITH AN ENGLISH GIRL AND COMPLETELY RECOVERED HIS MEMORY UPON HEARING HER NAME--*JEAN CASTEL*

NUSSERWANJI TATA (1822-1886) FATHER OF THE FOUNDER OF INDIA'S GREATEST INDUSTRIAL EMPIRE *WAS MARRIED AT THE AGE OF 4*

EMPEROR ANASTASIUS DICORUS
(430-518) of Byzantium, WHO ACQUIRED HIS CROWN BY MARRYING THE WIDOW OF EMPEROR ZENO, WON HER ATTENTION BECAUSE *ONE OF HIS EYES WAS BLUE AND THE OTHER BLACK*

THE **SMALL CHANGE** USED BY NATIVES OF MALEKULA IN THE NEW HEBRIDES, CONSISTS OF RED PLAITED MATS WITH FRINGES --*8 INCHES LONG*. PIGS ARE EXCHANGED FOR LARGER AMOUNTS

DANIEL BOONE (1734-1820) TO ESCAPE INDIANS PURSUING HIM, ONCE LEAPED ACROSS THE LITTLE MIAMI RIVER IN CLIFTON FALLS, OHIO --*A JUMP OF 22 FEET*

THE FLOWER PAGODA Wachet, Burma ITS DOME RESEMBLES A LOTUS FLOWER -- EVEN TO BEING PARTLY OPEN TO THE SKY

SCARECROWS in England FOR YEARS COMPRISED A *LARGE POTATO BRISTLING WITH SPARROW HAWK FEATHERS--FLUTTERING FROM A HIGH POLE*

RAPHAEL
(1483-1520)
ONE OF ITALY'S
GREATEST PAINTERS,
HAD A BRAIN
THAT WEIGHED
ONLY 41 OUNCES
--7/4 OUNCES LESS
THAN NORMAL

THE **CHURCH OF TINOS** in Greece,
IS VISITED ANNUALLY ON MARCH 25th BY
THOUSANDS OF PILGRIMS WHO BELIEVE
THAT THEIR ILLS WILL BE CURED BY
SLEEPING THAT NIGHT ON ITS FLOOR

" WHERE YOUR CRADLE STOOD,
THERE YOU SHALL REST
IN ETERNAL PEACE "

Epitaph TO ROSALIE LÖVINSON, WHO IS BURIED
IN THE JEWISH CEMETERY IN EAST BERLIN
--*ON THE VERY SPOT WHERE SHE WAS BORN.*
HER FATHER HAD BEEN THE CEMETERY
INSPECTOR, AND WHEN HIS HOME IN THE
CEMETERY WAS RAZED HE BOUGHT THE
LAND AS A FAMILY PLOT

TABLETS LONG CONSIDERED BY
NATIVES OF LEMNOS, GREECE,
AS AN ANTIDOTE AGAINST
ANY TYPE OF POISON,
WERE MADE BY MARKING
WITH THE SULTAN'S SEAL
*EARTH DUG FROM A
HILL CONSIDERED SACRED*

THE **DREAM** THAT PROVED
A FATAL PROPHECY !

JOHANN KASPAR LAVATER
(1741-1801)
PASTOR OF ZURICH, SWITZERLAND,
AUTHOR AND PHILOSOPHER,
DREAMT IN 1779 THAT HE HAD
BEEN SLAIN BY A BULLET.
20 YEARS LATER THE PEACEFUL
PASTOR WAS MORTALLY WOUNDED
BY A SOLDIER IN THE CAPTURE
OF ZURICH BY THE FRENCH

A **CRUDE OAK CHAIR**
PRESERVED IN THE
CATHEDRAL OF YORK,
ENGLAND, WAS
CONSTRUCTED IN
THE 7th CENTURY AND
*SERVED AS THE CORONATION
THRONE FOR KING RICHARD III
AND KING JAMES I*

THE FIRST USE OF BIOLOGICAL AND PSYCHOLOGICAL WARFARE!

HANNIBAL

(247-183 B.C.) THE CARTHAGINIAN GENERAL ENABLED KING PRUSIAS OF BITHYNIA TO WIN A GREAT NAVAL VICTORY OVER KING EUMENES OF PERGAMUM BY SUGGESTING THAT THE BITHYNIANS HURL ONTO THE DECKS OF THE ENEMY'S SHIPS *EARTHENWARE JUGS FILLED WITH VENOMOUS SNAKES!*

THE VEIL OF NEPTUNE
A MARINE ANIMAL IS SO CALLED BECAUSE ITS MANY STEMS LOOK LIKE REMNANTS OF A LACE VEIL

St. Columba's Cathedral in Londonderry, North Ireland, IS THE ONLY CHURCH EVER CONSECRATED AS BOTH A PARISH CHURCH AND A CATHEDRAL ON THE *SAME DAY!* (1633)

THE SIGNATURE
of CHIEF TUHAWAIKI of New Zealand (1805-1844) WHICH HE SIGNED TO ALL OFFICIAL DOCUMENTS *WAS A COPY OF THE ELABORATE TATTOO ON HIS FACE*

PAPER MONEY
WAS ISSUED IN 1862 BY THE CHEROKEE INDIANS

THE WRITING BOOKS
USED FOR THEIR HOMEWORK BY MANY CHILDREN IN JUNGLE VILLAGES IN INDIA *CONSIST OF PALM LEAVES WHICH OPEN IN THE SHAPE OF A FAN*

THE **BROTHERS WHO WERE ALIKE IN BOTH BIRTH AND DEATH!**
THE HOTTINET QUADRUPLETS
GIOVANNI, PIETRO, FRANCESCO AND GIUSEPPE
WERE BORN IN NAPLES, ITALY, IN 1841, AND
DIED AT INTERVALS OF 21 YEARS
GIOVANNI DIED IN 1862 AT THE AGE OF 21 AND
WAS JOINED IN DEATH BY PIETRO IN 1883,
FRANCESCO IN 1904 AND GIUSEPPE IN 1925

CHARLES LOUIS COCKE
(1820-1901) PRESIDENT OF
HOLLINS COLLEGE, VIRGINIA,
SERVED IN THAT POST FOR 54 YEARS
*WITHOUT RECEIVING A
CENT IN SALARY*
IN DEBT TO ITS PRESIDENT BY
$151,253 IN 1900, THE ENTIRE
COLLEGE WAS DEEDED TO HIM

GUINAN WOMEN of the Philippines
USE THE SAME TYPE OF WICKER
BASKETS AS HANDBAGS
-- AND HATS

**THE CHURCH OF
SANTA MARIA DELLA SALUTE**
in Venice, Italy,
CONSTRUCTED IN THE 17th CENTURY
TO EXPRESS APPRECIATION FOR THE
CESSATION OF A PLAGUE THAT KILLED
46,000 VENETIANS, STANDS IN A
MARSHY AREA ATOP MORE THAN
1,000,000 PILES

THE **MACABRE MEMORIAL**
THE MONUMENT
in Brest, France,
TO R.P. LEVACHER, WHO
SERVED AS FRENCH
CONSUL IN ALGERIA,
IS THE UP-ENDED
BARREL OF THE 23-
FOOT CANNON INTO
WHICH LEVACHER'S
BODY WAS STUFFED
IN 1683
-- *AND FIRED AT
THE FRENCH FLEET*

MONARCH WHO RULED IN CHAINS!
CALIPH DHAHER (1172-1226) of Baghdad,
WHO HAD BEEN IMPRISONED BY HIS FATHER FOR
19 YEARS BEFORE HE INHERITED THE CROWN,
HAD BECOME SO ACCUSTOMED TO HIS CHAINS
*THAT HE DONNED THEM FROM
TIME TO TIME ON THE THRONE!*

AN OUTDOOR ALTAR
erected in Valencia, Spain,
DURING A RELIGIOUS
FESTIVAL IS MADE
ENTIRELY OF FLOWERS

The Pipe
SIR WALTER
RALEIGH SMOKED
ON THE SCAFFOLD
JUST BEFORE HE
WAS BEHEADED
*IS STILL
USABLE
355 YEARS
LATER*

THE U-461, A GERMAN SUBMARINE,
WAS DESTROYED IN THE BAY OF BISCAY IN 1943
BY A BRITISH SUNDERLAND PLANE
-THE NUMBER OF WHICH WAS U-461

A GIANT BUDDHA
AT YUNG HO KUNG LAMASERY
in Peiping, China,
60 FEET HIGH,
*WAS CARVED FROM THE TRUNK
OF A SINGLE TREE*

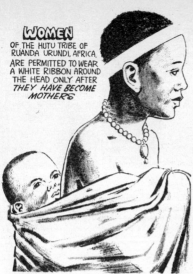

WOMEN OF THE HUTU TRIBE OF RUANDA URUNDI, AFRICA, ARE PERMITTED TO WEAR A WHITE RIBBON AROUND THE HEAD ONLY AFTER *THEY HAVE BECOME MOTHERS*

THE **MOST REMARKABLE SOMNAMBULIST IN ALL HISTORY!**
ADELAIDE HUS (1734-1806) THE FRENCH ACTRESS, GAVE A REPEAT PERFORMANCE OF HER STAGE ROLES, INCLUDING EVERY WORD AND GESTURE, WHILE SOUND ASLEEP --*NIGHTLY FOR 29 YEARS!*

THE **BELFRY** OF THE CHURCH OF PELLWORM ISLAND IN NORTH FRIESLAND, GERMANY, ALTHOUGH REDUCED TO A PERILOUS RUIN, HAS BEEN LEFT STANDING TO COMMEMORATE ITS POSITION FOR CENTURIES AS A *SANCTUARY TO ANY FUGITIVE*

THE **HARD PILLOW PLANT** OF TASMANIA GROWS IN THE SHAPE OF A PILLOW AND IS SO TIGHTLY ENTWINED *IT RESISTS EVEN THE THRUST OF A KNIFE BLADE*

HERE LIES ONE WHOSE LIFE'S THREAD CUT ASUNDER, SHE WAS STRUCK DEAD BY A CLAP OF THUNDER

Epitaph of Marcy Haile, Glastonbury, Conn. 1719

CHARLEMAGNE'S BEDSTEAD HIGH VENN DISTRICT OF BELGIUM
A HUGE BOULDER SHAPED LIKE A COUCH -- ON WHICH EMPEROR CHARLEMAGNE ONCE RESTED

THE EMPEROR WHO WAS A SERVANT IN HIS OWN HOUSEHOLD!
EMPEROR CHAO HUANG (939-997) of China ALTHOUGH HIS PALACE WAS STAFFED BY THOUSANDS OF EMPLOYEES, INSISTED ON PERSONALLY COOKING 5 MEALS A DAY FOR HIS MOTHER--AS WELL AS SERVING HER, SETTING THE TABLE AND WASHING HER DISHES-- FOR 40 YEARS
HIS OWN MEALS WERE PREPARED AND SERVED BY DOZENS OF ATTENDANTS

LUIGI TINELLI
(1798-1873) an Italian WAS SENTENCED TO DEATH FOR SUBVERSION IN AUSTRIA BUT THE SENTENCE WAS COMMUTED AND HE WAS GIVEN THE CHOICE OF 20 YEARS IN PRISON OR EMIGRATING TO AMERICA
HE BECAME AN ATTORNEY IN NEW YORK AND WAS LATER APPOINTED U.S. CONSUL IN OPORTO, PORTUGAL

THE KLAMATH LAKE SCULPIN
A FISH OF THE UPPER KLAMATH LAKE, IN OREGON, IS FOUND NOWHERE ELSE IN THE WORLD

THE PYRAMID SHAPED SIGNS
MARKING THE ANCIENT PILGRIMS' ROUTE TO LOP NOR, IN CENTRAL ASIA, WERE MADE OF WOOD --YET DESPITE THE REGION'S VIOLENT SANDSTORMS, THEY HAVE STOOD FOR 400 YEARS

THE CATHEDRAL OF SANTA MARIA MATRICOLARE
in Verona, Italy,
BUILT IN 1187 ON THE SITE OF AN ANCIENT ROMAN TEMPLE TO MINERVA --WAS CONSTRUCTED FROM THE DEBRIS OF THE ORIGINAL EDIFICE

SIGNATURE OF THE NOTORIOUS CAPTAIN KIDD

THE MARRIAGES THAT ALWAYS GO UP IN SMOKE!
A BRIDE AND GROOM IN THE TEMIAR TRIBE OF KELANTAN, MALAYA, ARE CONSIDERED LEGALLY WED WHEN FIRST THE MAN AND THEN THE WOMAN *PUFFS A CIGARET*

WILLIAM HUSKISSON
(1770-1830)
THE BRITISH STATESMAN
WAS THE WORLD'S FIRST VICTIM OF A RAILROAD ACCIDENT.
HE WAS FATALLY INJURED BY THE LOCOMOTIVE WHILE ATTENDING THE OPENING CEREMONY OF THE LIVERPOOL AND MANCHESTER RAILWAY IN SEPTEMBER, 1830

SPOONS ARE MADE BY THE BETSIMISARAKAS OF MADAGASCAR, *BY INGENIOUSLY FOLDING LEAVES*

THE STONE DEMONS Liboch, Czechoslovakia *NATURAL STONE FORMATION*

CAVE DWELLINGS in Nicosia, Sicily, WITH FACADES WHICH MAKE THEM RESEMBLE *TRADITIONAL HOUSES*

HE HAS ANSWERED HIS LAST ALARM

EPITAPH OF FIRE CAPT. WILLIAM P. MONROE, KILLED ON HIS WAY TO A FIRE, WILMINGTON, N.C.

The **GOLDEN ARM** IN THE CHURCH OF ST. NICOLAS-DU-PORT, FRANCE, CONTAINS A FINGER FROM THE HAND OF SANTA CLAUS

THE **WORKING ELEPHANTS** of Mysore, India, LABOR ONLY 4 HOURS A DAY AND ARE GUARANTEED BY LAW **3 MONTHS** OF VACATION EACH YEAR

TIBETAN MEN ALWAYS WEAR AN EARRING IN THE BELIEF THAT THE MALE WHO DOES NOT WILL BE REINCARNATED AS **A DONKEY**

THE **FLOATING VILLAGES OF VANCOUVER** VILLAGES CONSISTING OF A DOZEN COTTAGES, A MAIN STREET, A POSTOFFICE, A STORE AND A SCHOOLHOUSE, LOCATED ON **LARGE BARGES OFF THE COAST OF BRITISH COLUMBIA**

A DEATH CROWN WAS ONCE PLACED ON THE COFFIN OF ANY WOMAN WHO DIED SINGLE IN THURINGIA, GERMANY --AS COMPENSATION FOR NEVER HAVING WORN A BRIDAL WREATH

THE MERRY WIDOWER THE **BARON de LONGUEVILLE** (1780-1890) of Paris, France, WAS MARRIED 5 TIMES AFTER HE WAS **70** --TAKING HIS LAST BRIDE AT THE AGE OF **110**

THE COUNT de PARIS, A FRENCH CRUSADER, KNEELING IN AUDIENCE BEFORE EMPEROR ALEXIS I, OF BYZANTIUM, SUDDENLY AROSE AND ORDERED THE RULER TO MAKE ROOM FOR HIM ON THE GOLDEN THRONE, EXPLAINING: "MY FEET HURT!" THE EMPEROR MADE NO MOVE TO PUNISH THE CRUSADER FOR HIS AUDACITY (1096)

QUEEN FOR A DAY! INGELBURGA (1176-1236) THE SISTER OF KING CANUTE VI of Denmark WOOED BY KING PHILIPPE-AUGUSTE OF FRANCE, WHO HAD BEEN ASSURED SHE WAS BEAUTIFUL, MARRIED HIM IN 1193 AND WAS CROWNED QUEEN OF FRANCE --BUT HE ORDERED HER IMPRISONED AND STARTED A DIVORCE ACTION THE FOLLOWING MORNING

THE WEEKEND CHURCH OF SEOUL, Korea, HOLDS SERVICES REGULARLY FOR 13 DIFFERENT DENOMINATIONS

THE HOTEL OF MATMATA, TUNISIA, IS CONSTRUCTED INSIDE A CAVE

DUCKWEED THE SMALLEST FLOWERING PLANT IN ALL NATURE, IS ONLY AS BIG AS THE HEAD OF A PIN

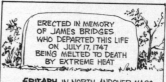

ERECTED IN MEMORY OF JAMES BRIDGES WHO DEPARTED THIS LIFE ON JULY 17, 1747 BEING MELTED TO DEATH BY EXTREME HEAT

EPITAPH IN NORTH ANDOVER, MASS.

NOEL NATIVIDAD NOEL
1635-1684
WAS BORN INTO A FAMILY NAMED
CHRISTMAS ON CHRISTMAS DAY,
TO A MOTHER WHO HERSELF WAS BORN
ON CHRISTMAS DAY.
HIS NAME MEANS
CHRISTMAS, CHRISTMAS, CHRISTMAS.
WE WISH ALL OUR READERS
A THRICE-BLESSED *Merry Christmas*

THE KALAMBO WATERFALL in Tanganyika, Africa, IS 880 FEET HIGH *BUT LESS THAN A YARD WIDE.* NATIVES CONSIDER IT A TEST OF COURAGE TO LEAP ACROSS IT

COMANCHE
A HORSE RIDDEN BY AN
OFFICER OF THE U.S. 7th CAVALRY,
*WAS THE ONLY SURVIVOR OF
THE CUSTER MASSACRE.*
IT HAD BEEN WOUNDED 7 TIMES, BUT
LIVED ANOTHER 15 YEARS

A DRIED APPLE
FOUND IN 1908, IN AN OAK
COFFIN IN SWEDEN,
STILL RETAINED ITS SHAPE
AFTER 3,500 YEARS

THE DOORS
OF THE TEMPLE OF MACHENDRANATH, NEPAL,
ARE SOLID SILVER

THE MOUNTAIN OF HEAVEN
HIGHEST ELEVATION IN DENMARK,
IS ONLY 482 FEET ABOVE SEA LEVEL

HAYSTACKS IN KIANGSI PROVINCE, CHINA, ARE SUSPENDED FROM TREES IN THE BELIEF IT ENHANCES THE LANDSCAPE

THE DOCTOR WHO MADE KNIGHTLY HOUSE CALLS
DR. SIEGMUND GOTZKIRCHNER OF MUNICH, GERMANY, PRACTICING MEDICINE FROM 1442 TO 1475 AT A TIME WHEN PHYSICIANS WERE OFTEN ATTACKED BY ROBBERS, MADE ALL HOUSE CALLS MOUNTED ON A HORSE, CLAD IN FULL ARMOR AND CARRYING A SWORD AND BATTLE AXE

THE MONASTERY OF IALOMICIOARA IN RUMANIA, IS LOCATED IN A CAVE IN THE CARPATHIAN MOUNTAINS

A BRONZE PENNY ISSUED IN ERROR BY THE AUSTRALIAN MINT IN 1930 SOLD FOR $400

ONE PENNY

THE BAKWIRI OF WEST AFRICA PLAY TUNES BY BLOWING ON THE STRING OF A BOW AND HITTING THE STRING WITH A STICK

THE KENNEL HOUSE
A WOMAN BEGGAR OF MESHED, IRAN, LIVED HER ENTIRE ADULT LIFE IN A DOG KENNEL THE SIZE OF A PACKING CASE

CLAUDE CHAUVEAU-LAGARDE
(1756-1841)

THE LAWYER WHO RISKED HIS OWN LIFE DEFENDING MARIE ANTOINETTE BEFORE THE REVOLUTIONARY TRIBUNAL, WAS ORDERED TO TURN OVER TO THE TRIBUNAL THE FEE HE RECEIVED *IN THE BELIEF HE HAD BEEN PAID AN ENORMOUS SUM*

HE PROMPTLY SENT THE TRIBUNAL HIS ONLY FEE - *A LOCK OF THE QUEEN'S HAIR* (Oct. 1793)

A **PALACE** BUILT IN ROME, ITALY, BY PIETRO RIARIO, AND STILL USED AS A GOVERNMENT OFFICE BUILDING WAS FINANCED BY $60,000 WON IN A SINGLE CARD GAME (1471)

THE **POISONOUS CENTIPEDE** of the Holy Land WHICH GROWS TO A LENGTH OF 6¾ INCHES *CARRIES ITS VENOM IN ITS LEGS*

THE SHIP THAT FOUND ITS WAY HOME!

THE **DORA**, A WHALER FROM PORT TOWNSEND, WASHINGTON, CONVERTED INTO A STEAMER BY THE ALASKA STEAMSHIP LINES, LOST HER ANCHOR AT COLD BAY, ALASKA, DRIFTED WITHOUT POWER OR COMPASS AND *ENDED UP 92 DAYS LATER AT HER OLD HOME PORT IN WASHINGTON*

HAULED OUT OF THE WATER, SHE WAS FOUND TO HAVE MADE THE VOYAGE WITH HER HULL STOVE IN--KEPT AFLOAT ONLY BY A ROCK IMBEDDED IN THE GAPING HOLE

ISLAND OFF THE COAST OF SOUTH CAROLINA *SHAPED LIKE A BEGGING BEAR* DRAWN FROM A PHOTO TAKEN FROM A PLANE BY NICK D'ERRICO OF NORTH HAVEN, CONN.

MINIATURES of a sacred pagoda on the banks of the Kaveri River, India, ARE CARVED OUT OF THE SNOW-WHITE PITH OF A MARSH PLANT THAT GROWS ON THE RIVERBANK

THE NOBLEMAN WHO BOUGHT HIS LIFE WITH A HANDFUL OF COINS!

AUGUSTE D'OYRON of Kerraud, France,
SENTENCED TO DEATH BY A REVOLUTIONARY TRIBUNAL
AND KNEELING IN FRONT OF AN EXECUTION SQUAD OF 4
SOLDIERS, SUDDENLY RIPPED OFF HIS BLINDFOLD AND
TOSSED IN THE AIR ALL THE GOLD HE WAS CARRYING
IN HIS POCKET -- *25 GUINEAS*

THE SOLDIERS SCRAMBLED FOR THE MONEY
AND D'OYRON ESCAPED INTO THE NIGHT --
SURVIVING FOR ANOTHER 42 YEARS (July 2, 1795)

WINTON C. PHIPPS
of Independence, Va.,
GROUSE HUNTING,
BAGGED A BIRD WHEN
IT FLEW STRAIGHT INTO
THE BARREL OF HIS GUN
-- *BREAKING ITS NECK*

THE **LEAF**
OF THE
GMELIN AGAR
*IS PERFORATED
LIKE A SIEVE*

THE **STICKLEBACK** a fish WHICH BUILDS ITS NEST AT THE BOTTOM OF A RIVER, FRIGHTENS OFF PREDATORS *BY STANDING ON ITS HEAD*

THE **REV. JAMES PRICE** (1756-1850) WHO WAS RECTOR OF 2 PARISHES IN WALES FOR 66 YEARS, INSISTED HE WAS SICK EVERY DAY OF THAT TIME -- *YET HE LIVED TO THE AGE OF 94*

NATURE'S BAROMETER
MOUNT BAR, AN EXTINCT VOLCANO NEAR MONLET, FRANCE, *ALWAYS GIVES WARNING OF A RAINSTORM* - WHEN A CLOUD FORMS ABOVE ITS PEAK NATIVES SAY, "MOUNT BAR HAS DONNED ITS RAINHAT"

THE **HEART URCHIN** LIVES IN A CHAMBER DUG INTO THE SEA BOTTOM AND BREATHES THROUGH 2 TUBES --*ONE COMING FROM ITS BACK AND THE OTHER FROM ITS TAIL*

HOUSE IN 2 COUNTRIES
THE HOME OF THE LATE JOHN MOORE NEAR SWEETGRASS, MONTANA, *HAS ITS BEDROOM IN THE UNITED STATES AND ITS KITCHEN IN CANADA*

THE SHOEMAKER WHOSE LIFE WAS SAVED BY A BIRTHMARK!

IGNACIO CUEVAS, A SHOEMAKER WHO HAD BEEN SENTENCED TO THE GALLOWS FOR A POLITICAL CRIME, WAS PARDONED BY THE COUNT DE REVILLAGIGEDO, THE SPANISH VICEROY OF MEXICO, WHEN THE HUMBLE DEFENDANT REVEALED

HE WAS THE VICEROY'S FATHER

BY RECALLING THAT THE COUNT HAD THE MARK OF A DOVE ON HIS RIGHT ARM THE SHOEMAKER PROVED HE HAD PLACED THE VICEROY IN AN ORPHANAGE AFTER HIS WIFE HAD DIED IN CHILDBIRTH--LEAVING HIM WITH 16 OTHER CHILDREN
1789

AXES
USED BY THE MARONENE TRIBE OF THE ISLAND OF CELEBES, INDONESIA, *ARE MADE FROM THE SHOULDERBLADES OF A BUFFALO*

THE SWIFTEST MASTER ARTIST IN HISTORY
ROELOF KOETS (1650-1725) CELEBRATED DUTCH ARTIST *PAINTED 5,000 PORTRAITS OF NOTABLES*
HIS PAINTINGS TODAY HAVE A TOTAL VALUE OF
$500,000,000

THE HIGHEST PAID ACTOR IN ALL HISTORY

APOLINARIS, a Roman stage player,
WAS CONSIDERED SO TALENTED BY EMPEROR VESPASIANUS
THAT HE WAS AWARDED BY THE RULER A SALARY OF
$400,000 A NIGHT !

DOGS ON TUAMOTU,
IN THE PACIFIC,
ARE TRAINED TO
CATCH FISH

POINT DUFOUR
HIGHEST SUMMIT OF
THE SWISS ALPS,
IS SHAPED LIKE
*THE HEAD OF
A LION*

A **DOG GAUGE**
WAS USED IN
MEDIEVAL ENGLAND
BY DOGCATCHERS
WHO MEASURED ANY
CANINE FOUND NEAR
THE ROYAL DEER
FORESTS AND
*LAMED ANY DOG
TOO LARGE TO
PASS THROUGH
THE GAUGE SO IT
COULD NOT HARM
THE DEER*

**CONVOLUTA
PARADOXA**
A WORM, *IS BOTH
AN ANIMAL AND A
PLANT AND BOTH
MALE AND FEMALE—
IT LAYS EGGS, EXISTS
BY PHOTOSYNTHESIS,
AND IS SO TINY
436,000 FILL ONLY ONE
CUBIC INCH OF SPACE*

72

AN **AQUAMARINE** FOUND IN CENTRAL BRAZIL WEIGHING 143 POUNDS --324,700 CARATS
Owned by Manoel Bento Dos Santos, of Guanabara, Brazil

CHARLEY BOSWELL a BLIND GOLFER PLAYING AT THE VESTAVIA COUNTRY CLUB, IN BIRMINGHAM, ALABAMA, *MADE A HOLE-IN-ONE*

THE LAMA TEMPLE OF SHERGOL in Tibet
IS CARVED OUT OF THE FACE OF A SHEER CLIFF IN AN AREA SO BLEAK THAT THERE IS NO VEGETATION AS FAR AS THE EYE CAN SEE

THE **CHESSBOARD FLOWER** HAS ON EACH PETAL THE DESIGN OF A *CHESSBOARD*

Epitaph OF JAMES EWINS IN FOREST HILL CEMETERY, EAST DERRY, N.H.
THE EPITAPH WAS INTENDED TO READ:
MY GLASS IS RUN

MY GLASS IS RUM

Here lies
JOE RACKET
IN HIS
WOODEN JACKET
HE KEPT NEITHER
HORSES NOR MULES
HE LIVED LIKE
A HOG
HE DIED LIKE
A DOG
AND LEFT ALL HIS
MONEY TO FOOLS

Epitaph in Woodton, Norfolk, England

THE CURSE THAT WAS FULFILLED AFTER 255 YEARS!

SIR ANTHONY BROWNE (1500-1548) WHO WAS GIVEN BATTLE ABBEY, IN ENGLAND, BY KING HENRY VIII, WAS WARNED BY THE MONKS WHO WERE EXPELLED FROM THE ABBEY THAT HIS FAMILY LINE WOULD BE WIPED OUT *BY FIRE AND WATER!*

HIS LAST MALE DESCENDANT, THE 8th VISCOUNT MONTAGUE, DROWNED IN 1793 AND IN THE SAME WEEK THE ANCESTRAL CASTLE OF COWDRAY BURNED TO THE GROUND!

IN 1903, TWO BOYS, DESCENDANTS OF THE MATERNAL SIDE OF THE FAMILY, DROWNED IN BOGNOR, ENGLAND

The QUEEN of HEARTS

QUEEN MARGUERITE (1553-1615) of Navarre, DAUGHTER OF KING HENRY II, OF FRANCE, AND DIVORCED WIFE OF FRANCE'S KING HENRY IV, WORE A WIDE HOOPSKIRT WITH 34 CONCEALED POCKETS --IN EACH OF WHICH SHE CARRIED A BOX CONTAINING THE *EMBALMED HEART OF A FORMER LOVER*

THE WATERFALL BIRD

THE DIPPER OFTEN BUILDS ITS NEST BEHIND A WATERFALL TO PROTECT IT FROM ALL PREDATORS *BECAUSE ONLY THE DIPPER FLIES THROUGH A WATERFALL*

SELLING A STICK OF CINNAMON IN DUTCH-RULED CEYLON WAS FOR 138 YEARS A CRIME PUNISHABLE *BY DEATH* (1658 - 1796)

NATURE'S TOTEM POLE
REFLECTION OF HILLMAN AND WATCHMAN PEAKS,
IN CRATER LAKE, OREGON
(TURN PAGE TO RIGHT UNTIL "TOTEM POLE" IS VERTICAL)
Submitted by Mrs. Lola Hunt, Cathedral City, Calif.

THE **LITTLE GIANT!**
DAVID RITCHIE (1740-1811)
immortalized by Sir Walter Scott as "The Black Dwarf"
WAS ONLY 3½ FEET TALL
— YET HE WAS SO STRONG THAT HE COULD
*PULL LARGE TREES FROM THE GROUND
WITH HIS BARE HANDS*

JOHN I. BLAIR
(1802-1899)
THE RAILROAD
BUILDER,
FOUNDED 80 TOWNS
*AND SUPPORTED
100 CHURCHES
IN THEM*

THE **CHURCH of SANTA MARIA MAGGIORE**
LAST REMAINING STRUCTURE OF THE ANCIENT
TOWN OF SIPONTUM IN APULIA, ITALY,
IS STILL USED FOR SERVICES BY LOCAL
FARMERS ALTHOUGH THE TOWN ITSELF
HAS BEEN ABANDONED FOR MORE THAN
700 YEARS

THE **QUEEN** WHO HAD A
WOODEN CHEST!
JANE SEYMOUR,
3d *WIFE OF KING HENRY VIII,*
TO COMPLY WITH THE DICTATES
OF FASHION, WORE ACROSS HER
CHEST BENEATH HER GOWN
A CURVED BOARD

75

THE **ANCIENT ARMENIANS** DELIVERED WINE TO BABYLON BY TRAVELING DOWN THE EUPHRATES RIVER *IN CIRCULAR LEATHER BOATS*

FOR THE RETURN TRIP THE LEATHER BOAT COVERING WAS LOADED ON A DONKEY --WHICH THEY ALWAYS BROUGHT ALONG AS PART OF THEIR ORIGINAL CARGO

PEASANTS IN OLD WESTPHALIA (Germany) KNEADED THE DOUGH FOR PUMPERNICKEL BREAD *BY TREADING ON IT WITH BARE FEET*

A JUG 12 FEET HIGH MADE BY CEMENTING TOGETHER **2,500 GLASS BOTTLES** Created by JAMES A. BARTLETT, Sultana, Calif.

THE **FIRST FAMILY** OF **MEDICINE**

DR. HERMAN URSINUS (1661-1738) of Halle, Germany, A PHYSICIAN, WAS THE FATHER OF DR. HEINRICH URSINUS DR. RUDOLF URSINUS DR. LUDWIG URSINUS DR. FRIEDRICH URSINUS DR. LUDOLF URSINUS DR. JOHANN URSINUS DR. PETER URSINUS DR. GEORG URSINUS DR. JAKOB URSINUS DR. SIEGFRIED URSINUS DR. KURT URSINUS DR. JOST URSINUS DR. KARL URSINUS --14 *PHYSICIANS IN ONE FAMILY!*

THE REMARKABLE OLD WOMAN OF WILEY!

Margery Brider (1530-1643)
of Wiley, England,
WHIRLED AND HIGH-STEPPED CONTINUOUSLY
FOR **4** HOURS IN A STRENUOUS FOLK DANCE
AT THE AGE OF 112

RAINBOW LAKE

A VOLCANIC CRATER LAKE ON THE WEST COAST OF LANZAROTE IN THE CANARY ISLANDS,

BECAUSE OF LAYERS OF LAVA CONSTANTLY DISPLAYS **6** *DIFFERENT COLORS*

THE **ALTAR** of the CONGREGATIONAL CHURCH OF RICHMOND, MASS., WHICH DISAPPEARED AFTER FIRE DAMAGED THE EDIFICE IN 1882, WAS RETURNED TO THE CHURCH IN 1950 --AFTER HAVING SERVED FOR 68 YEARS AS A COUNTER IN A STORE IN WEST PITTSFIELD, MASS.

THERESE ZOTTL

21-YEAR-OLD DAUGHTER OF A LABORER IN KUFSTEIN, AUSTRIA,

WAS SO BEAUTIFUL THAT WHEN HER PICTURE APPEARED IN A BERLIN, GERMANY, NEWSPAPER IN 1886 THE PAPER'S MILLIONAIRE PUBLISHER, AUGUST SCHERL, *FELL IN LOVE WITH IT AND MARRIED HER*

THE LEANING TOWER OF ST. JACOB

in Leeuwarden, Netherlands

LEANS 24 INCHES OFF CENTER

A LONG-HORN OX
FOUND IN THE KALAHARI DESERT OF AFRICA BY WILLIAM OSWELL, A COMPANION OF THE FAMED DR. LIVINGSTONE, *HAD HORNS 13½ FEET LONG*
ITS HORNS WERE SO HUGE THEY PREVENTED THE OX FROM REACHING THE GROUND TO FEED, SO ONLY ITS HORNS WERE BROUGHT BACK TO ENGLAND

PAPA I'M COMING

Epitaph OVER THE GRAVE OF GEORGE MERWIN WHO DIED AT 9, ON APRIL 10, 1876 Orange, Conn.

"HEARTS AND FLOWERS" the famous tear-jerker, WAS WRITTEN BY MARY BRINE

THE TRIANGULAR CHURCH OF PLANES
France,
WAS BUILT IN THAT SHAPE BY A PHILANTHROPIST TO SAVE TIME BECAUSE HE HAD BEEN WARNED BY HIS DOCTOR
THAT HE HAD ONLY ONE YEAR TO LIVE !
HE SURVIVED FOR NEARLY 40 YEARS .

IPOKRITOS
FROM WHICH THE ENGLISH "HYPOCRITE" IS DERIVED, *ORIGINALLY WAS THE WORD FOR AN ACTOR OF ANCIENT GREECE*

THE **TEMPLE OF THE DOOMED** !
A HINDU TEMPLE
near Karachi, Pakistan, WITH A SYMBOLIC GALLOWS ATTACHED TO ITS SANCTUARY, HONORS THE MEMORY OF ALL THOSE CONDEMNED TO HANG - ALTHOUGH THEY WERE INNOCENT !

A **BRIDE** of the Vakkaliga Tribe in India,
MUST BRING HER HUSBAND, AS A DOWRY, *THE FIRST JOINTS OF 2 FINGERS OF HER MOTHER'S RIGHT HAND !*
IT REPRESENTS AN IRREVOCABLE CONSENT TO THE MARRIAGE

THE HERCULES MOTH
THE LARGEST MOTH
MEASURES 14 INCHES FROM
WING TIP TO WING TIP—
ITS SPAN AS A MOTH IS
ONLY 14 DAYS AND
*IT EATS NOTHING
DURING THAT PERIOD*

**A HUMAN
FOOTPRINT**
FOUND IN THE
CAVE OF ALDENE,
FRANCE,
IS 40,000
YEARS OLD

THOMAS McKEAN (1734-1817)
A PRESIDENT OF THE CONTINENTAL
CONGRESS AND A SIGNER OF THE
DECLARATION OF INDEPENDENCE,
WAS CHIEF JUSTICE OF PENNSYLVANIA
FOR 22 YEARS, *AND DURING
THAT SAME PERIOD* SERVED
AS GOVERNOR OF DELAWARE
AND AS AN ASSEMBLYMAN AND
CONGRESSMAN FROM DELAWARE

**IRON
"TRIDENTS"**
THE ROYAL EMBLEM OF
18th CENTURY RULERS
OF NYASALAND, WERE
FOUND BURIED WITH THEM

AN IDOL
IN TAHITI,
CARVED FROM
*THE VERTEBRA
OF A MAN*

WILLIAM WILLIS, AT THE AGE OF 61,
SAILED ALONE FROM CALLAO, PERU, TO THE ISLAND OF
SAMOA—6,700 MILES IN 115 DAYS ON A RAFT (1954)

THE MEN WHO CHIP ROCKS
WITH THEIR TEETH !

THE
ABORIGINES
of the Gibson Desert of Australia
ARE THE ONLY PEOPLE ON EARTH WHO
CREATE STONE TOOLS AND WEAPONS BY
SHAPING ROCKS WITH THEIR TEETH !

SQUASH 36 INCHES LONG, **12½** INCHES
THICK, AND WEIGHING **9½** POUNDS
Grown by **I. M. Feldman**
Washington, D.C.

THE
**GEOMETER
MOTH**
of Australia
BLENDS SO
PERFECTLY
WITH THE
GRAIN OF ANY
WOOD THAT IT
IS INVISIBLE

THE DOOR OF THE BRIDEGROOM
IN THE CHURCH OF ST. GEORGE, IN PALOS, SPAIN,
IS OPENED ONLY FOR WEDDINGS IN THE PINZON
FAMILY--DESCENDANTS OF MARTIN ALONSO PINZON,
OWNER AND CAPTAIN OF ONE OF THE SHIPS
*ON THE VOYAGE, IN 1492, IN WHICH
COLUMBUS DISCOVERED AMERICA*

THE CHURCH OF OUR LADY OF THE END OF THE EARTH
in Soulac, France,
CONSTRUCTED IN 980 ON A WIND-SWEPT BEACH
*WAS UNUSABLE, AND, IN FACT, INVISIBLE
FOR 100 YEARS BECAUSE IT WAS
ENGULFED BY SAND*
IN 1859 A WINDSTORM BLEW THE SAND AWAY
AND THE CHURCH RESUMED SERVICES

A **SOLID SILVER COIN**
MINTED IN MEXICO CITY IN 1536
*--THE FIRST COIN MINTED
IN THE AMERICAS*

BEEF BONES
BEARING INSCRIPTIONS,
WERE USED BY THE CHINESE,
IN THE 15th CENTURY, TO
*PREDICT THE FUTURE, AND
GIVE THEM COUNSEL*

THE STATUE THAT FRIGHTENED ITS CREATOR TO DEATH!

THE "DEAD ONE",
A SKELETON-
LIKE STATUE,
NOW IN THE
CHURCH OF
ST. AUGUSTINE,
IN LIMA,
PERU,
WAS CARVED
IN THE 18th
CENTURY BY
BALTAZAR
GAVILAN—
WHO
STUMBLED
INTO IT
ONE NIGHT
IN HIS
STUDIO, AND
WAS SO
TERRIFIED
BY ITS
APPEARANCE
THAT HE
*SUFFERED
A FATAL
HEART
ATTACK*

MAN WITH A TOOTHACHE
WELLS CATHEDRAL, ENGLAND.
FOR YEARS IT WAS BELIEVED THAT
THINKING ABOUT THIS CARVING
COULD CURE A TOOTHACHE

THE **STRANGEST** PUNISHMENT FOR INFIDELITY!
PADAUNG WIVES OF BURMA, WHO HAVE BEEN UNFAITHFUL TO THEIR HUSBANDS, MAY BE FORCED TO REMOVE THE COPPER COILS THEY WEAR AROUND THEIR NECKS -- WHICH IS EQUIVALENT TO A DEATH SENTENCE BECAUSE THE NECK MUSCLES HAVE ATROPHIED AND *CANNOT SUPPORT THE VICTIM'S HEAD*

A **WINE CUP** SHAPED LIKE A ROMAN MILITARY BOOT WAS USED BY THE ANCIENT ROMAN GARRISON IN THE GERMAN RHINE COUNTRY IN THE BELIEF THAT DRINKING FROM IT *COULD CURE ANY FOOT AILMENT*

THE **MOST INTREPID RACE IN MARITIME HISTORY**
14 SMALL SAILING VESSELS, EACH CARRYING ONLY ONE MAN, SET OUT FROM PLYMOUTH, ENGLAND, JUNE 19, 1964, ON A RACE ACROSS THE OCEAN TO NEWPORT, RHODE ISLAND. THE HAZARDOUS CONTEST WAS WON BY LIEUT. ERIC TABARLY OF THE FRENCH NAVY, WHO ARRIVED IN 27 DAYS, 3 HOURS, 56 MINUTES

HOHAN SOKAN OF KOZA CITY, OKINAWA, HOLDER OF A 10th DEGREE BLACK BELT IN KARATE -- *THE HIGHEST RANK*-- STILL TEACHES KARATE AT THE AGE OF 87
Submitted by GEORGE A. DILLMAN, READING, PA.

AN **OAK** and a **PINE** GROWN TOGETHER NEAR HEINRICHSHAGEN, GERMANY, *TO FORM A SINGLE TREE*

THERE IS A TIME WHEN GREEN TREES SHALL FALL AND ISAAC GREENTREES RISE ABOVE THEM ALL

Epitaph in Harrow Churchyard, England

THE "FAITHFUL MAN"!
PHILIP RAMSEY
(1875-1922)
WHO LOVED THE ISLAND
OF MAN, ON WHICH
HE WAS BORN,
SUCCESSIVELY MARRIED
3 WOMEN NAMED
MARGARET ANN NAPIER
MILLIE AMALIA NAISMITH
AND
MARTHA AUGUSTA NEWTON

NEWS HOUND
A DOG DELIVERED "THE DAILY
TELEGRAPH" TO SUBSCRIBERS
IN YARMOUTH, ENGLAND (1869)

THE WOMEN'S SICKLE
of the Mandara
Tribe in the
No. Cameroons,
Africa,
WHICH ALSO
SERVES AS
LEGAL
TENDER,
CANNOT BE USED
BY A MAN.
AS MONEY
IT IS WORTH
2 CHICKENS

THE POST OFFICE BUILDING
IN KAKTOVIK, ON BARTER ISLAND IN THE ARCTIC OCEAN,
WAS SHIPPED TO THE SITE FROM FAIRBANKS, ALASKA,
BY AIR MAIL
Submitted by Dr. Ralph B. Williams, Juneau, Alaska

JULIA MAMMAEA
WAS
THE NIECE OF A
ROMAN EMPEROR
THE COUSIN OF A
ROMAN EMPEROR
THE AUNT OF
ANOTHER AND
THE MOTHER OF A
ROMAN EMPEROR

STEPHEN HOPKINS (1707-1785)
ONE OF THE SIGNERS OF THE
DECLARATION OF INDEPENDENCE,
WAS ELECTED GOVERNOR OF RHODE
ISLAND 10 TIMES

ALWAYS FIRM BUT EVER MILD
I NEVER SAW HER STRIKE A CHILD

Epitaph OF ANN, WIFE OF I. H.B., WHO DIED IN
1870, AGED 44 -- GUILFORD, IND.

MOUNT HÖFATS near Oberstdorf, Germany, IS THE ONLY MOUNTAIN IN THE COUNTRY ON WHICH EDELWEISS STILL GROWS

A SANDSTONE CARVING DEPICTING A KISS --FOUND IN THE 2,000-YEAR-OLD GRAVE OF A CHINESE SLAVE WHO CREATED IT AS A PROTEST AGAINST THE CHINESE BELIEF THAT PUBLIC KISSING IS OBSCENE

A WOODEN CART NOW IN THE HERMITAGE MUSEUM IN LENINGRAD, WAS FOUND IN THE ALTAI MOUNTAINS IN SIBERIA, 3,000 YEARS AFTER ITS CONSTRUCTION --PRESERVED BY THE PERMANENTLY FROZEN SOIL

"WRESTLING MATCHES" ARE STAGED BY THE MENANGKABAUS OF INDONESIA, BETWEEN 2 QUAIL

JOHANN QUANZ (1697-1773) THE GERMAN COMPOSER, WROTE 500 FLUTE CONCERTOS FOR KING FREDERICK THE GREAT OF PRUSSIA --WHICH NO ONE ELSE WAS PERMITTED TO PLAY

THE MAN WHO BECAME PRIME MINISTER BY A TRICK OF MAGIC!

FLAVITAS, A MAGICIAN of Byzantium in the 5th century, LEARNED THAT EMPEROR ZENO, SEEKING DIVINE HELP IN SELECTING A CHANCELLOR FOR THE EASTERN ROMAN EMPIRE, HAD PLACED A BLANK SHEET OF PAPER IN A SEALED CONTAINER.
BY SLEIGHT OF HAND FLAVITAS MANAGED TO GET HIS NAME ON THE PAPER - AND WAS NAMED TO THE HIGHEST OFFICE IN THE EMPIRE

THE MOST AMAZING MILITARY RECORD IN ALL HISTORY

ULRIC de LOWENDAL (1700-1755) A DANE

FOUGHT SUCCESSIVELY AS A

PRIVATE FOR POLAND

LIEUTENANT FOR DENMARK

CAPTAIN FOR HUNGARY

COLONEL FOR POLAND

COLONEL FOR PRUSSIA

LIEUTENANT GENERAL FOR RUSSIA

AND FINALLY AS A FRENCH FIELD MARSHAL

THE DUTCH TOWER in Bern, Switzerland, WAS GIVEN THAT NAME BECAUSE SWISS OFFICERS WHO LEARNED TO USE TOBACCO IN THE DUTCH WARS OF THE 16th CENTURY MET SECRETLY IN THE TOWER TO SMOKE -- *A VIOLATION OF THE LAW*

2 GET-WELL CARDS EXACTLY ALIKE RECEIVED BY MRS. ALMEDA YAUKEY, OF CHAMBERSBURG, PA., FROM 2 GRANDSONS WHO HAD MAILED THEM ON THE SAME DAY *FROM CITIES SEPARATED BY A DISTANCE OF 3,000 MILES*

CARP HAVE THEIR TEETH *IN THEIR THROAT*

THE RED INDIAN FISH OF AUSTRALIA IS SO NAMED BECAUSE IT BEARS A STRIKING RESEMBLANCE TO *AN AMERICAN INDIAN'S COLOR, FEATURES AND HEADDRESS*

THE PERFECT PLANNED FAMILY

WILLIAM COATES (1867-1914) OF London, England, WAS THE FATHER OF 13 CHILDREN NAMED

WINIFRED
IDA
LOUISE
LEO
IRMA
ANDERS
MITCHEL

CHARLES
ORVILLE
ALEXANDER
THOMAS
EVELYN
STEPHEN

INDIAN SQUAW WITH BASKET
Pyramid Lake, near Reno, Nev.
NATURAL STONE FORMATION
Submitted by Emery F. Tobin
Vancouver, Washington

THE SIGNPOSTS GUIDING CARAVANS THROUGH THE DESERT OF KHOTAN, IN THE PROVINCE OF SIN-KIANG, CHINA, *ARE PROPPED-UP SKELETONS OF CAMELS*

WOMEN OF THE BONDO TRIBE OF INDIA, WEAR JEWELRY WEIGHING **33 POUNDS**

REAL de CATORCE
A FORMER MINING TOWN IN MEXICO, IS THE ONLY COMMUNITY IN THE WESTERN HEMISPHERE THAT CAN BE *ENTERED ONLY BY A TUNNEL*

ABRAHAM FABERT
(1599-1662) A MARSHAL OF FRANCE,
UNWILLING TO DIE IN BED,
CRAWLED FROM HIS BED WHEN HE
REALIZED DEATH WAS IMMINENT,
AND DIED KNEELING IN PRAYER

FRIEDRICH von FLOTOW
THE GERMAN COMPOSER
OF OPERAS, WAS SO ADMIRED
BY A FRENCH MUSICIAN
NAMED FERNAND de FERNEY
THAT THE LATTER IMITATED
HIM IN DRESS, AND
IN HONOR OF VON
FLOTOW'S OPERA "MARTHA",
NAMED HIS 5 DAUGHTERS

MARTHA I
MARTHA II
MARTHA III
MARTHA IV
and
MARTHA V

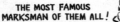

**THE MOST FAMOUS
MARKSMAN OF THEM ALL!**
ANDREW JACKSON (1767-1845)
THE GENERAL WHO BECAME THE
7th PRESIDENT OF THE U.S.,
FIRING A NEW PISTOL FOR THE FIRST TIME,
3 TIMES IN A ROW HIT, AT A DISTANCE
OF 40 YARDS, A TARGET CONSISTING
ONLY OF *2 CROSSED THREADS!*

THE MANDAU A SWORD USED BY THE DYAKS of BORNEO
IS BELIEVED TO BE MORE DEADLY IF ITS
POMMEL IS DECORATED WITH HAIR CUT FROM
THE HEAD OF A MAN IT HAS KILLED

JOHANN BRUNDGEN
(1840-1899)
OF MUNICH, BAVARIA,
AN ONLY CHILD,
BORN IN THE 21st
YEAR OF HIS PARENTS'
MARRIAGE, BECAME THE
FATHER OF A SON IN
*THE 21st YEAR OF
HIS OWN MARRIAGE*

**MARSHAL de
VIEILLEVILLE** (1510-1571)
HAVING CAPTURED THE
PRINCE de MELFI,
REJECTED A RANSOM
EQUIVALENT TO $5,820,000
BECAUSE OF HIS ADMIRATION
FOR THE PRINCE'S
COURAGE IN BATTLE
*--FREEING HIS PRISONER
FOR A RANSOM OF
ONLY 5 CENTS*

THE **TIGER CAVE** of Udayagiri, India,
*IS BELIEVED TO BE PROTECTED
FROM RODENTS BY A HUGE STONE
CARVING OF THE HEAD OF A TIGER*

THE **SNIPE**
IN ITS SWIFT
DESCENTS
MAKES A SOUND
LIKE THE
*BLEATING
OF A GOAT*

THE WOMAN WHO HEARD THROUGH HER MOUTH!

MADAME ISABELLE OREILLE
(1854-1899) A NOTED PIANIST OF PARIS, FRANCE,
WAS BORN WITHOUT EARS
--BUT COULD HEAR BY OPENING HER MOUTH!
SHE MARRIED A MAN NAMED OREILLE
-- THE FRENCH WORD FOR EAR

A MULBERRY TREE

IN THE GARDEN OF THE VAN JACOBS HOME IN GOES, NETHERLANDS,
GREW ON ITS TRUNK THE PROFILE OF A MAN'S HEAD
--WHICH LOCAL RESIDENTS INSIST RESEMBLES THAT OF
THE MR. VAN JACOBS WHO PLANTED IT

GARLIC PEDDLERS IN THE MARKET OF CAIRO, EGYPT, WEAR THEIR STOCK ON THEIR HEAD -- *A FRAGRANT COIFFURE*

HONCHO-DORI THE MOST ELEGANT STREET OF YOKOHAMA, JAPAN, IN THE 19th CENTURY, IS THE ORIGIN OF THE PHRASE *"HUNKY DORY"*--MEANING "EVERYTHING IS GREAT"

THE MOST FAMOUS TREE IN ALL HISTORY THE **TREE OF KURNAH** in Iraq, ON THE SITE OF THE BIBLICAL GARDEN OF EDEN, IS SAID TO BE THE TREE OF KNOWLEDGE *-- THE FRUIT OF WHICH PROVED TOO GREAT A TEMPTATION TO ADAM*

A **TOMATO PLANT** THAT IN ONE SEASON *PRODUCED 350 TOMATOES* Submitted by Franth Wetherholts, Mattoon, Ill.

THE MONASTERY OF PAULAR in Spain
WAS BUILT BY KING JUAN II
TO CURE HIS NIGHTMARES
THE SPANISH MONARCH REPEATEDLY RECALLED IN HIS
DREAMS DESTRUCTION OF A CARTHUSIAN MONASTERY BY
HIS GREAT-GRANDFATHER, KING ENRIQUE—AND CONSTRUCTION
OF A NEW MONASTERY BANISHED HIS NIGHTMARES

THE **SELIMIYE MOSQUE** OF NICOSIA, CYPRUS,
WAS CONVERTED INTO A MOSQUE BY THE TURKS
IN 1571, AFTER HAVING SERVED AS THE
CHURCH OF ST. SOPHIA FOR 163 YEARS

FISHERMEN IN COXYDE, BELGIUM,
CATCH SHRIMP AND FISH ON HORSEBACK

THE **LANGUAGE
OF THE LEAVES**
MESSAGES ARE SENT
BETWEEN NATIVES OF
THE NEW HEBRIDES ISLANDS
*BY CUTTING THE
LEAVES OF THE
SYCA TREE*
MUTILATION OF
SUCH A MESSAGE
OR INTERFERING
WITH ITS BEARER
WAS AT ONE TIME
PUNISHABLE BY
DEATH

WHERE WOMEN'S LIB IS LAW !
THE CUNA INDIANS of Panama
CELEBRATE THE BIRTH OF A GIRL WITH A JOYOUS
FEAST, DRESS THE CHILD IN FINERY, AND
PRESENT HER WITH A GOLD NOSE RING --
THE BIRTH OF A BABY BOY IS IGNORED--AND HE IS NOT
EVEN GIVEN CLOTHES UNTIL HE BECOMES AN ADULT

THE VAIN WOMAN
A *TREE* ON MARGARITA ISLAND, VENEZUELA,
THAT IS SHAPED LIKE A WOMAN
-- WITH HER HANDS RAISED
TO FLUFF HER COIFFURE

THE **SHARP SPUR** OF THE THICK UPPER LEG JOINT OF THE EURYCANTHA INSECT PROVIDES NATIVES OF THE GOODENOUGH ISLAND, IN NEW GUINEA, WITH A NATURAL FISH-HOOK

THE MAN WHO BECAME HIS OWN MEMORIAL!

THE LAST HOLY RULER of Mongolia, UPON HIS DEATH ON MAY 26, 1924, WAS EMBALMED AND COVERED WITH GOLD -- AND THE GOLDEN MUMMY STILL SITS IN THE PALACE AT ULAN BATOR ON THE THRONE THE RULER OCCUPIED IN LIFE

SACRED TO THE MEMORY OF
ANTHONY DRAKE
WHO DIED FOR PEACE AND QUIETNESS SAKE
HIS WIFE WAS CONSTANTLY
SCOLDING AND SCOFFIN
SO HE SOUGHT REPOSE
IN A TWELVE-DOLLAR COFFIN

Epitaph in Burlington, Mass., churchyard

THE OYSTER THIEF
A SEAWEED THAT IS BALLOON SHAPED AND FILLS WITH GAS FLOATS OUT TO SEA ON RISING TIDES, TAKING WITH IT YOUNG OYSTERS TO WHICH IT HAS BECOME ATTACHED

THE OLDEST ONE-WAY TRAFFIC SIGN

A SIGN STILL STANDING IN BARCELONA, SPAIN, WARNS DONKEY CARTS THEY MUST TRAVEL IN THE SAME DIRECTION AS THE ONE PICTURED ON THE SIGN --OR PAY A FINE OF 3 POUNDS-- IT WAS ERECTED IN THE 16th CENTURY

THE MAN WHO CAN TAME ARMIES OF VICIOUS ANTS!

PAULO KIBUGWE of Elizabethville in the Congo, A GRADUATE OF THE UNIVERSITY OF BRUSSELS, BELGIUM, WHO RETURNED TO HIS TRIBE, IS THE ONLY MAN IN THE ENTIRE WORLD WHO HAS LED CARAVANS SAFELY THROUGH HUNDREDS OF THOUSANDS OF DRIVER ANTS --AFRICA'S DEADLIEST SCOURGE. HIS PORTERS HAVE WALKED THROUGH SWARMS OF THE FEROCIOUS ANTS--BAREFOOTED!

THE BASILICA OF TRIER --Germany--

A PROTESTANT CHURCH SINCE 1844, WAS ORIGINALLY A PALACE OF ROMAN EMPEROR CONSTANTINE THE GREAT

GOLF'S FIRST FAMILY!

FRED J. PIEPER OF MURRAY HILL, N.J., A POLICE OFFICER AND ARDENT GOLFER, HAS 10 CHILDREN NAMED: FRED HAAS PIEPER, JIMMIE DEMARET PIEPER, BOBBY JONES PIEPER, DICK MAYER PIEPER, CAROL MANN PIEPER, SAM SNEAD PIEPER, PATTY BERG PIEPER, MICKEY WRIGHT PIEPER, BETSY RAWLS PIEPER, BEN HOGAN PIEPER

THE OFFICIAL EMBLEM

of Friedrichroda, Germany, IS A MAN'S FACE WITH HIS MOUTH OPEN --BECAUSE AFTER THE 30-YEARS' WAR SO FEW PEOPLE WERE LEFT THAT WHEN A STRANGER LEARNED HE WAS IN A TOWN HIS MOUTH DROPPED OPEN IN SURPRISE

THE MEDICINE MEN WHO NEVER FAIL TO COLLECT THEIR FEE!

A MEDICINE MAN OF THE HURI TRIBE OF NEW GUINEA,
WEARS A TOUPEE MADE FROM THE HAIR OF
PATIENTS WHO DIED UNDER HIS CARE

**HENRY
SANBORN
NOYES**
(1822-1872)
A MATHEMATICS
PROFESSOR AT
NORTHWESTERN
UNIVERSITY

MEMORIZED
THE ENTIRE
CONTENTS
OF HOMER'S
"ILIAD" AND
"THE ODYSSEY"

*--A TOTAL OF
162,000
WORDS*

THE BUILDING THAT BLUSHES
THE CHINESE ROCK TEMPLE OF IPOH
MALAYA
A FAÇADE COVERING A SERIES OF
MOUNTAIN CAVES, IS CREATED OF
WHITE ROCK-- BUT AT SUNRISE AS IT
REFLECTS THE RED LATERITE SOIL BENEATH
IT, *THE STRUCTURE APPEARS
TO BLUSH PINK*

THE PROPHECY THAT PROVED TRUE TO THE VERY INSTANT -- *AFTER 5 CENTURIES !*

THE TOMB OF TAMERLANE, in Samarkand, WAS OPENED BY A SOVIET SCIENTIFIC EXPEDITION AND HIS MUMMIFIED BODY WAS REMOVED AT **5 A.M. ON JUNE 22, 1941** DESPITE AN INSCRIPTION ON A HUGE BLOCK OF JADE THAT READ: *"IF I SHOULD BE BROUGHT BACK TO EARTH, THE GREATEST OF ALL WARS WILL ENGULF THIS LAND."*

AT THE SAME MOMENT, 2,500 MILES TO THE WEST, RUSSIA WAS INVADED BY 160 GERMAN DIVISIONS AND 14,000 TANKS *-- EMBROILING THE SCIENTISTS' HOMELAND IN THE GREATEST OF ALL WARS !*

THOMAS PRICE of Slatington, Pa., SHOT A HAWK IN THE AIR -- AND BROUGHT DOWN WITH IT *A RABBIT THE BIRD WAS CARRYING TO ITS NEST*

SHERIFF HENRY PLUMMER
OF BANNACK, MONTANA,
WHO WAS FOUND TO BE MOON-
LIGHTING AS A HIGHWAYMAN,
WAS HANGED ON A GALLOWS
HE HAD BUILT HIMSELF
FOR THE EXECUTION OF
A HORSE THIEF

THE LIVING BUDDHA OF KANZE
THE **LAMA** WHO RULES 7
LAMASERIES IN THE
HIMALAYA MOUNTAINS
SPENDS HIS ENTIRE LIFE-
TIME ON A TABLE TOP IN
AN OPEN TENT, SQUATTING
ON IT ALL DAY AND SLEEP-
ING ON IT AT NIGHT

THE ARCH OF TRAIAN
ERECTED AT THAMUGADI, ALGERIA,
TO HONOR THE ROMAN EMPEROR,
WAS REBUILT IN THE 19th CENTURY
FROM THE ORIGINAL MATERIALS
AFTER HAVING BEEN BURIED
IN THE SANDS FOR 1,000 YEARS

THE **FENCE** of the Hardscrabble Estate, in St. Louis, Mo.,
ERECTED AS A MEMORIAL TO ALL SOLDIERS
SLAIN IN THE CIVIL WAR, CONSISTS OF
THE BARRELS OF 2,000 RIFLES

THE **BRIDGE** of **LANDERNEAU**
in France
BUILT IN 1518
IS LINED WITH HOMES AND
A FLOUR MILL, ALL OF WHICH
HAVE BEEN OCCUPIED
CONTINUOUSLY FOR 453 YEARS

THE
BIER OF EACH
DECEASED RULER
OF THE KOTOKOS
OF AFRICA
--WHICH ALSO
SERVES AS THE
FIRST BED OF
EACH NEW RULER--
*IS AN OLD
WOODEN DOOR*

THE ALL-TIME PERFECT FAMILY !
AGENOR PAILLET (1880-1930) of Paris, France,
WAS ONE OF 4 CHILDREN--3 BROTHERS AND A SISTER:
AGENOR, *BORN DECEMBER 12,* 1880,
RAOUL, *BORN MARCH 11,* 1882,
JEAN, *BORN SEPTEMBER 4,* 1898,
AND DELPHINE, *BORN JANUARY 4,* 1902 -
AGENOR BECAME THE FATHER OF 3 BOYS
AND A GIRL, WHO WERE NAMED AFTER
THEIR FATHER, UNCLES AND AUNT
*-- EACH HAVING THE IDENTICAL
BIRTHDAY OF HIS OR HER NAMESAKE -*
AGENOR, *BORN DECEMBER 12,* 1904,-
RAOUL, *BORN MARCH 11,* 1906,
JEAN, *BORN SEPTEMBER 4,* 1909,
DELPHINE, *BORN JANUARY 4,* 1912

SOUTHERN CROSS
A FISH FOUND IN SAMOA
WAS GIVEN THAT NAME
BECAUSE ITS 4
PRINCIPAL PROJECTIONS
ARE IN THE SAME
RELATIVE POSITIONS AS
*THE 4 STARS COMPRISING
THE SOUTHERN CROSS*

THE **HYDRA**, a fresh-water polyp
PROPELS ITSELF ALONG BY
TURNING SOMERSAULTS

THE **NO.1** WORKING MAN OF THE WHOLE WORLD!

JEAN CAUSEUR (1640-1771) OF PLOUMOGUER, FRANCE WORKED AS A BUTCHER **FOR 101 YEARS!** *HE RETIRED AT THE AGE OF 121 AND LIVED TO BE 131*

GENERAL JULES TROCHU (1815-1896) WAS ELECTED TO THE FRENCH PARLIAMENT IN 1871 SIMULTANEOUSLY FROM 8 DISTRICTS *ALTHOUGH IN 1871 HE HAD BEEN THE MILITARY COMMANDER OF PARIS WHO SURRENDERED THE CITY TO THE GERMANS*

THE **EAST SIDE POST OFFICE** in Saginaw, Mich.
WAS DESIGNED AS A REPLICA OF THE ANCESTRAL
CASTLE OF THE DE TOCQUEVILLE FAMILY, IN MENOU, FRANCE
--*BECAUSE ALEXIS DE TOCQUEVILLE*
ONCE VISITED SAGINAW

RAJAH BUKHT
of Nagore and Jhallore, India,
WAS ASSASSINATED IN 1721 BY HIS NIECE
BY MEANS OF A SILKEN ROBE
THAT HAD BEEN SOAKED IN POISON

THE MAN WHO WAS LIVING PROOF
THAT BACHELORS LIVE LONGER!

SEBASTIÃO AGUILAR (1802-1902)
of Santarem, Portugal,
REFUSED TO MARRY BECAUSE HE WAS
THE POSTHUMOUS SON OF A POSTHUMOUS SON
OF A POSTHUMOUS SON

HIS FATHER, ANGELO, AND HIS GRANDFATHER,
ESTEVÃO, EACH DIED 5 MONTHS BEFORE THE BIRTH
OF HIS ONLY SON -- BUT SEBASTIÃO, A BACHELOR,
LIVED TO THE AGE OF 100

THE DECORATOR BIRD
THE MALE SATIN BOWER BIRD
ACTUALLY PAINTS THE WALLS OF ITS
BOWER NEST--*USING A FIBER BRUSH
DIPPED IN CHARCOAL AND SALIVA*

THE SOUTH AMERICAN LEAF FISH
FLOATS BENEATH THE
SURFACE OF THE WATER
*AND LOOKS EXACTLY
LIKE A LEAF*

MODERN APARTMENT HOUSES
in Barcelona, Spain,
OFTEN ARE BUILT WITH A WAVY FAÇADE
--TO EMPHASIZE THE CITY'S SEAPORT ATMOSPHERE

**THE FAMED CONCERT
PIANIST WHOSE MIND
WAS NEVER ON HIS WORK**
Ernst Lengyel von Bagota
(1893-1914)
ONE OF EUROPE'S MOST
CELEBRATED MUSICIANS,
INSTEAD OF PLACING MUSICAL
SCORES ON HIS PIANO RACK
SPREAD OUT A NUMBER
OF TIMETABLES
*--AND MEMORIZED THEM AS
HE PLAYED CONCERTS!*

THE **LEANING TOWER**
OF THE OLD CHURCH OF
ST. MORITZ, SWITZERLAND,
IS 16 INCHES OFF CENTER

MINIATURE HANDCUFFS
ARE WOVEN FROM RATTAN PALM FIBERS
BY THE HEADHUNTERS OF
CENTRAL CELEBES, INDONESIA,
*AS THEIR DOCUMENTARY
RECORDS OF WAR EXPLOITS*

RUDE BIRDS
THE **TURACOUS**
OF SO. AFRICA
CONSTANTLY CHIRP
"GO AWAY"

103

THE FRENCHMAN WHO LIVED TWO LIVES!
LOUIS-MARIA MESSIGNY (1742-1832)
A CHEF INJURED IN AN EXPLOSION IN HIS KITCHEN
BECAME AN AMNESIA VICTIM FOR 30 YEARS
--AND IN THAT PERIOD COMPOSED 31 OPERAS!
AT THE AGE OF 60 THE COLLAPSE OF A STAGE RESTORED HIS MEMORY AND
HE AGAIN BECAME A CHEF--UNABLE TO WRITE ANOTHER LINE OF MUSIC

SAMUEL JOHNSTON (1733-1816)
CONVINCED HE WAS UNWORTHY OF THE
HIGH POST, RESIGNED AS PRESIDENT
OF THE CONTINENTAL CONGRESS
AFTER SERVING FOR ONLY ONE DAY-
HE LATER WAS BOTH GOVERNOR OF
NORTH CAROLINA AND A U.S. SENATOR

Pearls
ARE FOUND IN
MUSSELS IN THE
RIVER VIERRE,
IN BELGIUM, AT
*INTERVALS OF ABOUT
EVERY 10 YEARS*

THE OLD MAN OF THE SEA!

WOLRAAD WOLTEMADE, AN ELDERLY RESIDENT OF CAPETOWN, SO. AFRICA, SAW THE
DUTCH SHIP "JONGE THOMAS", WITH 200 PASSENGERS ABOARD, FOUNDERING
IN A HEAVY STORM IN TABLE BAY -- AND WENT TO ITS RESCUE
ON A BORROWED HORSE!

7 TIMES HE RODE THROUGH THE RAGING SURF AND EACH TIME
BROUGHT BACK 2 MEN CLINGING TO HIS STIRRUPS -- BUT ON THE 8th
EFFORT BOTH WOLTEMADE AND HIS MOUNT PERISHED   (1773)

JACK OF ALL TRADES!

LOUIS-ARMAND JAEKEL
(1705-1773) of Paris, France,
*CHANGED HIS VOCATION
EVERY 10 YEARS*
HE BECAME A DANCING MASTER IN
1723, A PLAYWRIGHT IN 1733, BEGAN
PRACTICING MEDICINE IN 1743,
BECAME A LAWYER IN 1753, AN
ENGINEER IN 1763, AND AN AUTHOR
IN THE LAST YEAR OF HIS LIFE
*--AND WAS SUCCESSFUL
IN EACH FIELD*

THE NIAMOUS OF AFRICA'S IVORY COAST CROSS THEIR RIVERS ON BRIDGES BUILT BY MERELY *LASHING TOGETHER SCORES OF FLOATING LOGS*

X. NOEL of Nîmes, France, BECAME THE FATHER OF QUADRUPLETS ON **Christmas Day** --AND NAMED THEM: *HEUREUX* --MEANING HAPPY *FORTUNÉ* --MEANING FORTUNATE *FELIX* -- MEANING FELICITOUS and *GAI* FOR GAY

ELFRETH'S ALLEY IN PHILADELPHIA, PA. INHABITED CONTINUOUSLY SINCE 1736, *IS THE OLDEST RESIDENTIAL STREET IN THE UNITED STATES*

THE SALT PLANT THE PISTIA, WHICH GROWS IN THE BOGS OF EQUATORIAL AFRICA, IS DRIED AND BURNED BY PYGMIES AND ITS *ASHES YIELD SALT FOR THEIR FOOD*

Clarence A PEDIGREED BULLDOG SERVED AS A MARINE CORPS SERGEANT AND WAS ISSUED A UNIFORM, SERIAL NUMBER, STRIPES AND JUMP WINGS *HAVING MADE A 1,500-FOOT PARACHUTE JUMP* Owned by Sgt. Major A.D. Clark (Ret.) Twentynine Palms, Calif.

THE **PLAGUE** WAS COMBATED BY THE BHAR TRIBE, of India, BY DRIVING A YOUNG WATER BUFFALO THROUGH THE VILLAGE WHILE NATIVES CREATED A TREMENDOUS DIN *--TO FRIGHTEN THE EPIDEMIC INTO THE BODY OF THE BUFFALO*

THE MARBLE CHURCH of Copenhagen, Denmark, DESIGNED AS A REPLICA OF ST. PETER'S IN ROME IN 1749, WAS LEFT UNFINISHED FOR 100 YEARS WHEN ITS BUILDERS RAN OUT OF MONEY AFTER SPENDING THE EQUIVALENT OF **$1,350,000**

THE **RANGOON CREEPER** IS CALLED *"THE HEART OF MAN"* **BECAUSE IT IS SO CHANGEABLE** ITS COLOR CONSTANTLY SWITCHES FROM RED TO WHITE

BERNARD RENAU (1652-1719) A FRENCH NAVAL OFFICER WHO CAPTURED AN ENGLISH SHIP CARRYING $800,000 WORTH OF DIAMONDS AND PRESENTED THEM TO THE FRENCH KING ALTHOUGH THEY WERE LEGALLY HIS, WAS AWARDED A PENSION EQUIVALENT TODAY TO **$36,000 A YEAR**

A **CONVERTIBLE TABLE** USED IN MANY AMERICAN HOMES IN COLONIAL TIMES *DOUBLED AS A CHAIR*

THE CLUBHOUSE
OF THE MARTINDALE COUNTRY CLUB,
IN AUBURN, MAINE,
WITHOUT ONCE CHANGING ITS SITE
HAS BEEN LOCATED IN
2 STATES - MAINE AND MASSACHUSETTS -
2 COUNTIES - CUMBERLAND AND ANDROSCOGGIN -
ONE CITY - AUBURN - and
3 TOWNS - AUBURN, DANVILLE AND POLAND
Submitted by RALPH B. SKINNER
Auburn, Me., City Historian

**MR. and MRS. EDD
HOLLEN**
of Bear Branch, Ky.,
CELEBRATED THEIR
*83d WEDDING
ANNIVERSARY*
THEY WERE
MARRIED
MAY 7, 1889

A *LIGHT BULB* IN THE HEADQUARTERS OF
THE LIVERMORE, CALIFORNIA, FIREHOUSE
HAS BURNED ALMOST CONTINUOUSLY
FOR 71 YEARS
Submitted by Michael R. Dunstan
Livermore Herald and News

ST. BARBARA'S ALTAR
in the Church of St. Joseph, in Zabrze, Poland,
A MINING COMMUNITY,
IS MADE ENTIRELY OF COAL

CLAUDE FRANÇOIS MENESTRIER
(1631-1705) TAUGHT ORATORY AT
TRINITY COLLEGE, IN LYON, FRANCE,
WHEN HE WAS ONLY
15 YEARS OF AGE
HE HAD SUCH A FANTASTIC MEMORY
THAT AFTER HEARING 300 ARTIFICIALLY
CONCOCTED WORDS HE RECITED THEM
BACK WITHOUT AN ERROR-- *AND
THEN DID IT AGAIN IN
REVERSE ORDER*

THE **GOLDEN DAGGER**
of Hallstatt, Austria,
WAS FOUND IN A GRAVE IN
WHICH IT HAD BEEN BURIED
MORE THAN 3,000 YEARS –
THE BLADE WAS FUSED BY RUST TO THE
SCABBARD WHEN IT WAS DISCOVERED IN 1858,
BUT 98 YEARS LATER AN ELECTROLYTIC PROCESS
MADE IT POSSIBLE TO REMOVE THE DAGGER

THE ROUND CHURCH OF ST. STEPHEN
in Rome, Italy,
HOLDS SERVICES ONLY ONCE EACH YEAR
ON *ST. STEPHEN'S DAY--DECEMBER 26th*

THE **THRONE**
OF DINGAAN,
KING OF THE
ZULUS FROM
1828 TO 1840,
WHICH IS
PRESERVED IN
JOHANNESBURG,
So. AFRICA,
*IS A 3-LEGGED
CHAIR CARVED
FROM A SOLID
BLOCK OF WOOD*

THE **CORYPHA
GEBANGA
PALM**
of Sumatra
NEVER BLOOMS
OR BEARS
FRUIT UNTIL
IT IS 50
YEARS OLD
--AND
*THEN
DIES*

THE **MOST AMAZING DEMONSTRATION OF
CONCENTRATION IN ALL HISTORY**

LAMBERT THOMAS SCHENKELS
(1547-1630) A COLLEGE PROFESSOR
OF 's HERTOGENBOSCH, NETHERLANDS,
AS DRAMATIC PROOF OF HIS MEMORY AND
POWER OF CONCENTRATION,
*DICTATED SIMULTANEOUSLY TO 20
SECRETARIES ON 20 DIFFERENT SUBJECTS
IN 12 DIFFERENT LANGUAGES-*
HE ALTERNATELY DICTATED 6 LINES
AT A TIME TO EACH SECRETARY

**ADDISON
H.
DAY**
AN OFFICER
OF A NEW
YORK BANK,
COMMUTED FROM
HIS HOME IN
CHATHAM, N.J.,
TO HIS OFFICE
*EVERY WEEKDAY
FOR 64 YEARS
AND 11 MONTHS*

CATS WERE TRAINED BY
THE ANCIENT EGYPTIANS
AS RETRIEVERS IN HUNTING BIRDS

THE CHILD WHO KILLED A MAN-EATING LIONESS!

MENGO, A 10-YEAR-OLD BOY OF THE TORO TRIBE IN AFRICA TRACKED DOWN A LIONESS WHICH HAD KILLED AND CARRIED OFF HIS FATHER **AND PLUNGED A SPEAR INTO ITS CHEST** *THE LIONESS ROLLED OVER ON THE WEAPON--AND ITS OWN WEIGHT CAUSED THE SPEAR TO PENETRATE ITS HEART* (1894)

A **SINGLE LEAF** of the Alocasia Macrorrhiza Plant IS SO LARGE THAT IT IS USED BY MALAY WOMEN AS A *SCREEN TO PROVIDE PRIVACY WHEN THEY BATHE*

THE BULLDOG ANT OF AUSTRALIA IS AN EXCELLENT SWIMMER AND ENJOYS A DAILY BATH

THE **NEST** OF THE LANCEOLATE HONEY EATER OF AUSTRALIA IS CONSTRUCTED AS A HAMMOCK *WHICH SWINGS FROM A BRANCH OF THE MYAL TREE*

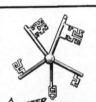

A **CLUSTER** OF **5 KEYS** USED IN THE 17th CENTURY--JOINED BY A PIVOT WHICH ENABLED THE USER *TO FOLD THEM TOGETHER OR SPREAD THEM APART*

THE CHURCH OF ST. SALVATOR
IN GMÜND, GERMANY, INCLUDING ITS 2 CHAPELS, WINDOWS, PULPIT AND DOORWAY, *WAS CARVED FROM SOLID ROCK*
ITS BELFRY WAS CONSTRUCTED NORMALLY AT A LATER DAY

THE WOMAN WHOSE BEAUTY IS PROCLAIMED BY THE STARS
QUEEN BERENICE III, WIFE OF KING PTOLEMY III, OF EGYPT, AS A SACRIFICE TO VENUS TO ASSURE HER HUSBAND'S SAFE RETURN FROM WAR, *CUT OFF HER HAIR AND DEPOSITED IT IN A TEMPLE.*
WHEN IT DISAPPEARED MATHEMATICIAN CONON GALLANTLY TOLD THE QUEEN HER HAIR HAD BEEN PLACED AMONG THE STARS-- *AND A CONSTELLATION STILL BEARS THE NAME, BERENICE'S HAIR*

ROSE BUSH
TRANSPLANTED 5 TIMES IN 3 STATES
-- YET HAS BLOOMED ANNUALLY FOR 76 YEARS
Submitted by HENRY M. HARPER, Delray Beach, Fla.

THE FEATHERED "BIRD DOG"
THE CAGOU, A BIRD FOUND ONLY ON THE ISLAND OF NEW CALEDONIA, *CANNOT FLY AND BARKS LIKE A DOG*

POTTERY
DISCOVERED ON THE SITE OF THE BIBLICAL CITY OF MIZPAH, IN THE HOLY LAND, REVEALED THAT POTTERS 3,000 YEARS AGO SIGNED THEIR WORK *WITH A FINGERPRINT*

THE MOST AMAZING SLEEPWALKER IN ALL HISTORY

ÉTIENNE de CONDILLAC (1715-1780)
THE FAMED FRENCH PHILOSOPHER,
WHILE SERVING AS TUTOR TO THE GRANDSON
OF KING LOUIS XV, OF FRANCE, WROTE A
13-VOLUME COURSE OF STUDY FOR HIS PUPIL
-- *MOST OF IT IN HIS SLEEP!*
MOREOVER, THE HUNDREDS OF PAGES OF
PHILOSOPHY, HISTORY AND GRAMMAR,
WRITTEN AS A SOMNAMBULIST, COULD NOT
BE DISTINGUISHED FROM THE WORK DONE
WHILE HE WAS AWAKE

ORANGES
FOR FOUR
CENTURIES
*WERE FORBIDDEN
FRUIT IN SPAIN
TO INFIDELS*
FOR A NON-MOOR
THE PENALTY FOR
EATING AN ORANGE
WAS DEATH

MILK CARTS
ON THE ISLAND OF
ST. MIGUEL, IN THE AZORES,
ARE DRAWN BY
HARNESSED, SHEEP

MONARCH OF THE NIMRODS
KING FERDINAND IV (1751-1825)
RULER OF NAPLES FOR 66 YEARS
*KILLED 1,820 WILD BOARS, 1,968 STAGS,
5 BEARS, 13 WOLVES, 7,121 RABBITS,
354 FOXES, 15,350 PHEASANTS, 1,625
GOATS, 16,354 HARES, 1,625 ROEBUCK
AND 12,435 PARTRIDGES*

A **HORSESHOE**
THROWN IN
A GAME OF
HORSESHOES
-- *BALANCED
ON TOP OF
THE STAKE*
Submitted by
Wilfred Pratte,
Pawtucket, R.I.

FARM HOUSES
IN SVANETIA, IN THE RUSSIAN CAUCASUS,
ARE STILL BUILT WITH STONE TOWERS
*BECAUSE FOR CENTURIES THE SVANETIANS
RELIED ON TOWERS TO DEFEND THEMSELVES
AGAINST ENEMY ATTACKS*

THE **PERCH** A FISH, REVEALS ITS
AGE BY THE NUMBER OF RINGS
ON ITS GILL COVERS

THE **MADONNA OF THE PEOPLE**
A REVERED STATUE IN THE CATHEDRAL
OF MONREALE, SICILY, WAS CARVED FROM
THE CAROB TREE BENEATH WHICH KING
WILLIAM II, OF SICILY, SAW A VISION
OF THE MADONNA IN A DREAM

BILAAN TRIBESMEN
in the Philippine Islands
WEAR TROUSERS EMBROIDERED
WITH THE SAME DESIGN
THEIR ANCESTORS DISPLAYED
ON THEIR LEGS IN THE FORM
OF TATTOOS

THE
**PORTUGUESE
FLY CATCHER
PLANT**
IS HUNG IN
PORTUGUESE HOMES
*AS A LIVING
FLY CATCHER*

113

THE CLOCK of DEATH

THE STEEPLE CLOCK OF THE CHURCH OF ALTOETTING, GERMANY, FEATURES A SKELETON WIELDING A SCYTHE BECAUSE IT WAS ERECTED IN 1648 *DURING THE GREAT PLAGUE*

THE MAN WHO BECAME HIS OWN MEMORIAL

A MONUMENT IN THE MONASTERY OF EXALTED HEAVEN, IN PEKING, CHINA, TO A MYSTERIOUS MONK WHO IS BELIEVED TO HAVE RULED CHINA AS EMPEROR SHUN CHI FROM 1644 TO 1661 *IS ACTUALLY HIS MUMMIFIED BODY --PLATED WITH GOLD*

THE EMPEROR IS BELIEVED TO HAVE RETIRED TO THE MONASTERY AFTER THE DEATH OF A BELOVED CONCUBINE

THE LARGEST DIOCESE IN HISTORY

WILLIAM GRANT BROUGHTON (1788-1853)

SERVED AS BISHOP OF ALL AUSTRALIA AND NEW ZEALAND *AN AREA OF 3,180,000 SQUARE MILES* HIS DIOCESE WAS DIVIDED IN 1847 INTO 6 BISHOPRICS

"ROLLIE" a PENGUIN IN THE SAN DIEGO, CALIF., ZOO, IS SO SKILLED ON ROLLER SKATES THAT HE WAS MADE *AN OFFICIAL MEMBER OF THE ROLLER SKATING ASSOCIATION*

CHIEFS ON THE ISLAND OF FLORES, INDONESIA, ARE INTERRED AFTER DEATH BY BEING WRAPPED IN FIBERS *AGAINST THE UPPER TRUNK OF A HIGH TREE*

THE **GRASS SKIRT** WHICH IS CONSIDERED SYMBOLIC OF HAWAII *DID NOT ORIGINATE IN HAWAII* IT WAS IMPORTED FROM THE GILBERT ISLANDS BY KING KALAKAUA, OF HAWAII, (1879-1891), WHEN HE REVIVED THE HULA DANCE

ELABORATE CHAIRS ARE CARVED BY THE NGONI OF CENTRAL AFRICA *ENTIRELY FROM A SINGLE BLOCK OF WOOD*

A **HUGE TORTOISE** IN PORT LOUIS, ON THE ISLAND OF MAURITIUS, *WALKED WITH 6 MEN ON ITS BACK* 1850

THE GATE OF ST. LO
IN THE CATHEDRAL OF COUTANCES, FRANCE, IS OPENED ONLY FOR THE ENTRY OF A NEW BISHOP
--AND FOR HIS FUNERAL

THE ELDEST SON
IN THE CHIN TRIBE OF UPPER BURMA,
UPON THE DEATH OF HIS FATHER,
*MUST MARRY ALL HIS FATHER'S WIDOWS
-- EXCEPT HIS OWN MOTHER --*
AND ALSO MUST WED THE YOUNGEST DAUGHTER
OF HIS FATHER'S OLDEST SISTER

AFRICAN WEAVER BIRDS
HAVE LEARNED TO ADJUST TO MODERN
TIMES -- ANCHORING THEIR NESTS TO TELEGRAPH
LINES WITH 10-FOOT FIBERS, *WRAPPED
AROUND THE WIRE TO PREVENT SLIPPAGE*

THE
"IMPULSORIA"
A LOCOMOTIVE
INVENTED BY
CLEMENTE MASERANO,
AN ENGINEER FROM
PISTOIA, ITALY,
AND SUCCESSFULLY
TESTED ON ENGLAND'S
SOUTHWESTERN
RAILWAY IN 1845
*WAS POWERED
BY 2 TEAMS OF
HORSES GALLOPING
ON A TREADMILL*

LEAVES OF THE BOMAREA CARDERI, OF CENTRAL AMERICA, TWIST AT INTERVALS SO THAT ALL SURFACES *GET EQUAL EXPOSURE TO THE SUN*

THE **CRYBABY FLOWER** THE CORAL TREE FLOWER WHEN CRUSHED EMITS A SOUND LIKE THAT OF A *WAILING BABY*

ISAAC BROCK
(1787-1909) of Waco, Texas
LIVED IN 3 CENTURIES
HE ENLISTED IN THE CONFEDERATE ARMY AT THE AGE OF 74 AND LIVED TO BE 122

THE 13th CENTURY DOOR OF THE CHURCH OF ST. MARTIN de LERIDA, SPAIN, WAS REMOVED AND INSTALLED IN THE CHURCH OF TORMILLO, THEN A CENTURY LATER BECAME THE ENTRANCE TO A PRISON, AND 200 YEARS AGO WAS RETURNED TO THE CHURCH OF ST. MARTIN *WHICH IT STILL SERVES TODAY*

THE ARTIFICIAL WATERFALL IN WILHELMSHÖHE PARK, KASSEL, GERMANY, WHICH CASCADES 141 FEET OVER A FAKE ROMAN RUIN, WAS CONSTRUCTED WITH FUNDS FROM ENGLAND -- *PAYMENT FOR HESSIAN SOLDIERS WHO FOUGHT IN THE AMERICAN REVOLUTION*

THE **SKULLS** OF 4 ANCESTORS
ARE DISPLAYED BY EACH CHIEF OF THE
KIBOSHO TRIBE OF TANZANIA
AS PROOF OF HIS ROYAL HERITAGE

A BRONZE MONUMENT
IN FRANKFORT-ON-THE-MAIN, GERMANY,
HONORS A HORSE THAT CARRIED ITS RIDER
TO SAFETY IN THE NAPOLEONIC WARS
*AFTER HE HAD FOUND HIMSELF
SURROUNDED BY FRENCH SOLDIERS*

**DR. JOHANN
CHRISTIAN
SENCKENBERG**
(1707 - 1772)
of Frankfort-on-the-
Main, Germany
WHO WAS WIDOWED
THREE TIMES
DIRECTED IN HIS
WILL THAT HIS
BURIAL SHROUD BE
*HIS FIRST WIFE'S
WEDDING GOWN*

THE **METROPOLITAN CATHEDRAL**
of Valencia, Spain,
WAS BUILT AS A HEATHEN TEMPLE TO
DIANA AND ALSO SERVED FOR YEARS
AS A MOHAMMEDAN MOSQUE

THE COMBER BEE
IT BUILDS THE ROOF OF ITS
NEST FROM GRASS AND MOSS
FIBERS WHICH IT PREPARES
*BY USING ITS 3 PAIRS
OF LEGS AS COMBS*

MARISCHAL COLLEGE, in Aberdeen, Scotland,
FOR CENTURIES HAS HAD AS ITS OFFICIAL MOTTO:
"LET THEM SAY WHATEVER THEY SAID"
IT ORIGINATED 3 CENTURIES AGO WHEN GEORGE KEITH,
WHO FOUNDED THE COLLEGE WITH MONEY OBTAINED
BY CONFISCATING ECCLESIASTICAL PROPERTY,
DISMISSED PROTESTS BY SAYING, "Let them talk"

THE MOST AMAZING GUIDE IN ALL HISTORY!
(1802-1882)
NICCOLO BABOCCHIO
WAS A PROFESSIONAL GUIDE IN THE MAREMMA, A MARSHY REGION OF ITALY IMPENETRABLE TO STRANGERS BECAUSE OF BOGS AND QUICKSAND
--*ALTHOUGH HE WAS BLIND FROM BIRTH!*
HE HAD 12 BLIND SONS, BUT EACH OF THEM BECAME SIGHTED BEFORE HE WAS 18

GOLD SWORDTAIL
WITH **2** HEADS
--*WHICH BOTH EAT*
Owned by John R. Post
Torrance, Calif.

SIR WILLIAM de la POLE
(1328-1366)
AS A REWARD FOR LENDING KING EDWARD III OF ENGLAND A SUM EQUAL IN PURCHASING POWER TODAY TO
$ 12,000,000
WAS GRANTED A LICENSE THAT WOULD PERMIT
HIS WIDOW TO REMARRY.
ENGLISH WIDOWS IN THE 14th CENTURY COULD MARRY AGAIN ONLY BY SPECIAL PERMISSION OF THE KING

THE MAN WHO FORETOLD HIS OWN DOOM TO THE HOUR!
GEORGE THALER of Gnadenwald, Austria,
PREDICTED IN 1643 THAT HE WOULD DIE
5 YEARS LATER AT 4 A.M. ON SEPT. 4th
*HE DIED OF NATURAL CAUSES AT 4 A.M. ON SEPT. 4, 1648 --
AND HIS PROPHECY IS INSCRIBED ON HIS TOMBSTONE*

THE READING ROOM
OF THE BRITISH MUSEUM, IN LONDON, ENGLAND,
DESIGNED BY ANTONIO PANIZZI, AN ITALIAN, IN 1857,
*HAS THE EXACT SHAPE AND DIMENSIONS OF THE
DOME OF ST. PETER'S BASILICA IN ROME*

THE **TELEPHONE PLANT**
OF PUERTO RICO
*GROWS ON
RUSTY IRON
WIRES*

THE **AUSTRALIAN
CHERRY TREE**
BEARS
FRUIT WITH
*THE PITS
ON THE
OUTSIDE*

THE MOST INHUMAN LAW OF ALL TIME!

EVERY MOTHER
OF NOBLE HERITAGE IN THE STATE OF
CHITRAL, INDIA, IN FORMER TIMES
SURRENDERED HER INFANT
IMMEDIATELY AFTER ITS BIRTH
*--AND RENOUNCED ALL KINSHIP
TO THE CHILD FOREVER!*
THE CHILDREN WERE BROUGHT UP BY
FOSTER PARENTS WHO HAD
NO BLOOD RELATIONSHIP

THE **INDIAN
CHIEF**

SUPERSTITION
MOUNTAINS
OF ARIZONA

*NATURAL
STONE
FORMATION*

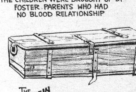

THE **COFFIN** THAT HELD 7,000 BODIES!
A SINGLE COFFIN
DURING AN EPIDEMIC IN
STAMMHEIM, SWITZERLAND,
IN 1611, WAS USED TO
TRANSPORT TO THE CEMETERY
7,000 VICTIMS
EACH BODY WAS DUMPED INTO
A MASS GRAVE THROUGH THE
COFFIN'S HINGED BOTTOM

THE MOST STUBBORN DUELIST
IN ALL HISTORY !

JEAN-LOUIS de SURVILLE (1760-1793)
CHALLENGED TO A DUEL TO THE DEATH,
INSISTED THAT BOTH ANTAGONISTS USE
THE SAME ANCIENT COATS OF ARMOR AND
BROADSWORDS EMPLOYED IN DUELS IN WHICH
*HIS FATHER, GRANDFATHER, GREAT-.
GRANDFATHER AND GREAT-GREAT
GRANDFATHER WERE SLAIN*
JEAN-LOUIS FAILED TO ACHIEVE A VICTORY
FOR HIS ANCESTRAL ARMOR -- BUT HE
AND HIS OPPONENT WERE RECONCILED

THE **SPIKED WAR CLUBS**
USED BY NATIVES OF POLYNESIA
WERE CARVED FROM THE TRUNK OF A PANDANUS PINE
--WITH A SECTION OF ROOT SERVING AS THE HEAD

HERE LIES DOUR DURAND
BENEATH A HARD STONE
HAS HIS SOUL BEEN SAVED?
NOBODY KNOWS AND
NOBODY CARES

Epitaph IN THE CEMETERY
OF THE CHURCH OF
ST. POURCAIN, FRANCE,
OVER THE GRAVE OF BISHOP
GUILLAUME DURAND
*WHO COMPOSED
IT HIMSELF*

GEORGE WASHINGTON
WAS A FRENCH CITIZEN

THE **SNOW** BRIDGE
OVER THE HEADWATERS OF THE RIVER DEE, SCOTLAND,
USUALLY REMAINS THROUGHOUT THE YEAR

DAVID W. PIPES
(1845-1939)
OF NEW ORLEANS, LA.,
AND HIS FATHER,
BETWEEN THEM,
LIVED UNDER EVERY
U.S. PRESIDENT FROM
WASHINGTON TO
FRANKLIN D. ROOSEVELT
--A TOTAL OF
31 PRESIDENTS

THE **MOST ASTOUNDING PERFORMER
IN THEATRICAL HISTORY!**
MARGARET CULTING (1722-1772)
BECAME AN ACTRESS IN LONDON, ENGLAND,
WITH EXCELLENT DICTION
*ALTHOUGH SHE WAS BORN
WITHOUT A TONGUE*

TEXTS
WRITTEN BY HAUSA TRIBESMEN OF
NIGERIA, ARE PENNED FROM THE
TOP OF THE SHEET TO THE BOTTOM
*--BUT THEY ARE READ BY TURNING
THE SHEET ON ITS SIDE AND
READING FROM RIGHT TO LEFT*

**THE MOST MODEST MULTI-MILLIONAIRE
IN HISTORY**
ALEXANDER AGUADO (1784-1842)
A FRENCH BANKER WHO DIED IN 1842
LEFT A FORTUNE EQUIVALENT
TODAY TO $120,000,000
*--YET IN HIS WILL HE APOLOGIZED TO
HIS FAMILY FOR HIS MEAGER ESTATE*

A
DOLL'S
CHAIR
CONSTRUCTED
IN GREECE
FROM
THE
BONES
OF A
GOOSE
2,400
YEARS
AGO

THE OLDEST ARCH IN THE WORLD
Ur of the Chaldees, Iraq,
AN ARCH
IN A RUINED CONVENT IN THE
HOMETOWN OF THE PATRIARCH ABRAHAM
BUILT BY THE DAUGHTERS OF
CHALDEAN KING NABONIDOS
2,500 YEARS AGO

WILLIAM QUARRIER
(1829 - 1903)
COLLECTED **$10,000,000**
TO BUILD 38 ORPHAN ASYLUMS,
7 SANATORIUMS AND A
HOME FOR EPILEPTICS
*WITHOUT EVER MAKING A
SOLICITATION FOR FUNDS*
QUARRIER RELIED ENTIRELY
ON PRAYER -- AND THE
DONATIONS ALWAYS ARRIVED
WHEN THEY WERE
NEEDED THE MOST
- Scotland

THE GLÜCKSBURG CASTLE - Germany -
WHICH DERIVES ITS NAME (*GOOD LUCK CASTLE*) FROM THE
HERALDIC MOTTO: "GOD GRANT GOOD LUCK AND PEACE"
*GAVE ITS NAME TO 3 EUROPEAN ROYAL DYNASTIES
-- THE KINGS OF DENMARK, NORWAY AND GREECE*

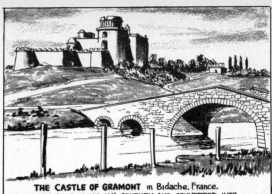

THE CASTLE OF GRAMONT in Bidache, France, WHICH WAS BUILT IN THE 11th CENTURY AND CONVERTED INTO A MILITARY HOSPITAL DURING THE FRENCH REVOLUTION, WAS BURNED DOWN IN 1794 BY ITS OWN SUPERINTENDENT -- *TO DESTROY EVIDENCE OF A SHORTAGE IN HIS ACCOUNTS*

THE COUNT de VERGENNES

RECEIVED A COMPLETE DOSSIER ON ALPHONS D'ANGEHA FROM THE MARQUIS DE PUYSEGUR, FRENCH AMBASSADOR IN LISBON, IN THE FORM OF CODED INDICATIONS ON A CARD OF INTRODUCTION

THE CARD REVEALED ITS BEARER WAS A PORTUGUESE, 45, TALL, HANDSOME, FRIENDLY, WEALTHY, A FORMER SOLDIER, EDUCATED, HONORABLE--AND IN LOVE

THE OCTAGON SHAPE OF THE CARD, WIDTH OF ITS BORDER, THE SUNFLOWER, SMALL CIRCLES AND OTHER FEATURES EACH HAD A HIDDEN MEANING

ALPHONS D'ANGEHA

RECOMMANDÉ A MONSIEUR LE COMTE DE VERGENNES PAR LE MARQUIS DE PUYSEGUR AMBASSADEUR DE FRANCE A LA COUR DE LISBONNE.

126

THE **SHOELACE WORM**
(Lineus Marinus)
LOOKS LIKE A
LOOPED PIECE
OF STRING

THE **LUNA MOTH**

IS CONSIDERED BY
MANY ENTOMOLOGISTS
*THE MOST BEAUTIFUL
INSECT IN
ALL NATURE*

THE BIRD THAT NAMED A COUNTRY'S RULER!

EMIR ALHAKEM

of Khorasan, Iran,
WAS HAVING DIFFICULTY CONVINCING THE STATE
COUNCIL TO NAME HIS 4th SON, ABDEL RAHMAN, AS
HIS SUCCESSOR, WHEN A STARLING SUDDENLY
FLEW IN A WINDOW, CIRCLED THE ROOM AND
TWICE PRONOUNCED THE NAME ABDEL RAHMAN!
ALHAKEM, AT A COST OF $4,800, HAD BOUGHT A
TALKING STARLING AND HAD IT TRAINED TO MAKE
THE FLIGHT AND SPEAK THE NAME OF HIS SON

THE **FLORIDA YEW**
WHICH GROWS ON THE
EASTERN SHORE
OF FLORIDA'S
APALACHICOLA RIVER

*IS FOUND NOWHERE
ELSE IN THE WORLD*

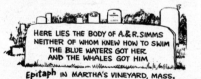

HERE LIES THE BODY OF A. & R. SIMMS
NEITHER OF WHOM KNEW HOW TO SWIM
THE BLUE WATERS GOT HER
AND THE WHALES GOT HIM

Epitaph IN MARTHA'S VINEYARD, MASS.

ALL HONEYBEES in the U.S.
*ARE DESCENDED
FROM IMMIGRANTS*
THE FIRST HONEYBEES WERE BROUGHT TO
THE U.S. FROM GERMANY IN 1638 AND OTHERS
WERE IMPORTED FROM ITALY IN 1855

THE WOMAN TO WHOM LOVE GAVE THE STRENGTH OF TWO MEN!

AMANDA SKIDDY IN CHARGE OF THE COMMISSARY OF THE 34th BRITISH REGIMENT IN THE PENINSULAR WAR, SAW HER HUSBAND DAN, AN INFANTRY PRIVATE, FALL WOUNDED DURING THE RETREAT FROM BURGOS, SPAIN, *WITH A HOPELESSLY SHATTERED LEG*— SHE LIFTED HER HUSBAND, HIS MUSKET, AND HIS HEAVY KNAPSACK *--AND CARRIED HIM 1½ MILES TO SAFETY (1808)*

JAMES F. BENSON WHO CAME TO ITAWAMBA COUNTY, MISS., AS A CHILD IN 1844, SERVED AS CIRCUIT CLERK AND TAX ASSESSOR, BUILT 8 BAPTIST CHURCHES *AND WAS PASTOR OF 20 CHURCHES*

BIRCH TREE BEARING ON ITS BARK THE FEATURES OF A MAN'S FACE

Submitted by Thomas Musoleno, Danbury, Conn.

THE **GRASS** OF **PARNASSUS** HAS STAR-LIKE FLOWERS WHICH HAVE NO SCENT AT NIGHT *--YET HAVE THE FRAGRANCE OF HONEY IN THE DAYTIME*

THE OLDEST WASHBASIN IN HISTORY

A BRONZE BASIN FOUND IN THE RUINS OF AN EGYPTIAN CITY, WAS USED BY THE BUILDERS OF THE PYRAMIDS AND *IS BELIEVED TO BE* 4,500 YEARS OLD

BERNARDO PUTAIRI

BECAME RULER OF THE GAMBIER ISLANDS, IN THE PACIFIC, IN 1872

BECAUSE, WHILE SERVING AS A COOK *HE BECAME THE OWNER OF THE DISCARDED UNIFORM OF A FRENCH COLONEL*

from an old print

THE TOWN THAT WAS SAVED BY BEES!

KISSINGEN, A TOWN IN GERMANY, DEFEATED AN ATTACKING ARMY IN 1643 *BY HURLING BEEHIVES AT THE ENEMY TROOPS -- WHO FLED IN TERROR*

THE TEXTBOOKS THAT WERE WRITTEN ENTIRELY FROM MEMORY!
CESARE MAJOLI (1746-1823) PROFESSOR OF THEOLOGY AT THE UNIVERSITY OF IMOLA AND FERRARA, IN ITALY, AND PROFESSOR OF PHILOSOPHY AT THE UNIVERSITY OF ROME, WROTE 27 VOLUMES ON BOTANY FROM MEMORY *AFTER HE HAD BECOME STONE BLIND!*

THE MOST DUTIFUL WIFE IN HISTORY
CALPURNIA
WIFE OF THE ROMAN AUTHOR, PLINY THE YOUNGER, AS EVIDENCE OF HER RESPECT FOR HER HUSBAND *MEMORIZED EVERY WORD HE EVER WROTE -- IN HIS PERSONAL LETTERS AS WELL AS HIS BOOKS*

THE BASKET TREE
THE YELLOW WILLOW TREE WAS INTRODUCED TO AMERICA BY BENJAMIN FRANKLIN, WHO PLANTED IN PHILADELPHIA *TWIGS BROKEN FROM A WILLOW BASKET IN WHICH MERCHANDISE HAD BEEN SHIPPED TO HIM FROM EUROPE*

BARMOUTH BRIDGE in Wales, WHICH IS A HALF-MILE LONG, IS HALF IRON AND HALF WOOD--BECAUSE *ITS BUILDERS RAN SHORT OF FUNDS*

THE RULER WHO FELT HE WAS FOOLING FATE!
SHAH ABBAS THE GREAT
(1557-1628) of Iran, A FIRM BELIEVER IN ASTROLOGY,
WAS WARNED **6** TIMES DURING HIS 41-YEAR REIGN
THAT THE STARS PREDICTED THE DEATH OF IRAN'S RULER
WITHIN THE MONTH
*EACH TIME HE TURNED OVER HIS THRONE TO A CRIMINAL
-- WHO WAS EXECUTED WITHIN A MONTH*

**THE CHURCH
OF BROU,**
France,
COMPLETED IN 1555
IN FULFILLMENT
OF A VOW
WAS CONSTRUCTED
AT A COST OF
2,200,000 FRANCS
*-- EQUIVALENT
TODAY TO
$11,000,000*

THE WATERFALL IN A CITY STREET
THE LEUKBACH, A TRIBUTARY OF THE SAAR RIVER, PLUNGES OVER A FALL AS IT RACES THROUGH *A NARROW STREET* OF THE TOWN OF SAARBURG, GERMANY

"SNAKE STONES"
FOSSIL SHELLS OF THE NAUTILUS WITH A SNAKE'S HEAD CARVED ON THEM, WERE SO POPULAR A SOUVENIR FOR YEARS IN WHITBY, ENGLAND, THAT THEY NOW *ADORN THE TOWN'S OFFICIAL COAT-OF-ARMS*

THE GENERAL WHO DIED ON HIS FEET!
PRINCE ERNEST von MANSFELD (1585-1626) A GERMAN SOLDIER AWARE THAT HIS LIFE WAS ENDING, DONNED HIS GENERAL'S UNIFORM AND DECORATIONS AND WITH TWO AIDES SUPPORTING HIM *DIED STANDING UP*

THE WORLD'S NO.1 FIRE BUFF
FIELD MARSHAL GIDEON von LAUDON (1716-1790)
COMMANDER-IN-CHIEF OF THE AUSTRIAN ARMIES
THROUGHOUT HIS MILITARY CAREER WOULD
BOLT FROM A MEETING OF THE GENERAL
STAFF AT THE SOUND OF FIRE BELLS --
TO HELP FIGHT THE BLAZE

THE **KILLDEER**
A SMALL BIRD
LAYS **4** EGGS
--THE COMBINED WEIGHT OF
WHICH EQUALS THE ENTIRE
WEIGHT OF THE MOTHER

A **MOOR'S FACE**
ON THE DIAL OF
A CLOCK IN
SZCZECIN
CASTLE, POLAND
*MARKS EACH
SECOND BY
ROLLING ITS
EYES*

THE **CIGAR
BEETLE**
IN BUILDING ITS NEST
ROLLS UP A LEAF IN THE SAME
WAY A CIGAR MAKER
ROLLS UP A TOBACCO LEAF

A **GIANT
TORTOISE**
TRANSPORTED FROM
THE GALAPAGOS ISLANDS
IN THE PACIFIC, TO MAURITIUS
IN THE INDIAN OCEAN,
SURVIVED ON MAURITIUS
FOR **152** YEARS

THE STOCK EXCHANGE
IN ROME, ITALY
*WAS ERECTED IN 138 A.D. AS A HEATHEN
TEMPLE TO HONOR EMPEROR HADRIAN*

LIEUTENANT Thomas W. Sweeny
WHO LOST HIS RIGHT ARM FIGHTING
WITH THE FIRST N.Y. VOLUNTEERS IN
MEXICO IN 1847, REMAINED IN THE ARMY,
SERVED THROUGHOUT THE CIVIL WAR,
AND RETIRED IN 1869 AS
BRIGADIER GENERAL

LORD BROUGHAM
(1778-1868)
THE BRITISH CHANCELLOR
DRANK SO MUCH BRANDY
DURING A LENGTHY
SPEECH IN 1832 THAT HE
INSPIRED THE EXPRESSION
" DRUNK AS A LORD "
*--AND A LIQUOR JUG
WAS DESIGNED IN
HIS LIKENESS*

CRICKET FIGHTS
ARE A LEADING SPORTS
EVENT IN CHINA, AND THE
WINNER MUST ALWAYS CHIRP
--OR BE DISQUALIFIED

THE COOKTOWN RAILWAY
IN Queensland, Australia,
OPERATED OVER 67 MILES
OF TRACK FOR 34 YEARS
USING AS ITS MOTIVE
POWER THE ENGINES
*OF SECONDHAND
AUTOMOBILES*

"THUNDERBOLTS" IS THE NAME FOR PETRIFIED BONES OF PREHISTORIC CUTTLEFISH BECAUSE IT WAS LONG BELIEVED THEY WERE THE *REMAINS FROM BOLTS OF LIGHTNING*

BDELLOSTOMA A FISH FOUND IN CALIFORNIA LAYS HOOKED EGGS WHICH LOCK INTO EACH OTHER TO FORM A CHAIN

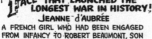

THE FACE THAT LAUNCHED THE LONGEST WAR IN HISTORY!

JEANNE d'AUBRÉE

A FRENCH GIRL WHO HAD BEEN ENGAGED FROM INFANCY TO ROBERT BEAUMONT, SON OF THE COUNT OF FLANDERS, MET HER FIANCE FOR THE FIRST TIME AT THE AGE OF 19 AND THE ENGAGEMENT WAS PROMPTLY BROKEN OFF BECAUSE SHE HAD *APPLIED MAKEUP TO HER FACE*

JEANNE'S COUSIN, KING PHILIP VI of France, BANISHED THE COUNT AND HIS SON, WHO THEN PERSUADED KING EDWARD III OF ENGLAND, TO INVADE FRANCE *-- STARTING THE 100-YEAR WAR THAT ACTUALLY LASTED FROM 1339 TO 1453!*

THE **FLY FLOWER** (Ophrys muscifera) HAS BLOSSOMS THAT APPEAR TO BE FLIES CLINGING TO ITS STEM

JARS WERE USED BY THE ANCIENT ISRAELITES TO COLLECT THE TEARS OF MOURNERS AT FUNERALS AND THEN PLACED IN THE GRAVE AS *PROOF OF THE SORROW AT THE LOSS OF THE DECEASED*

BOX CONTAINING 24 BASEBALLS

SAME BOX CONTAINING 25 BASEBALLS OF EXACTLY THE SAME SIZE

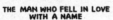

THE MAN WHO FELL IN LOVE WITH A NAME

RAMON BARROSO (1854 - 1911)
of Madrid, Spain,
MARRIED 4 TIMES
EACH TIME CHOOSING AS HIS BRIDE
A GIRL WHOSE MAIDEN NAME WAS
CATALINA GABINO
THEY WERE NOT RELATED

THE **CITY HALL OF OESTRICH**
Germany
WAS BUILT IN 1504 BY A DISGRUNTLED ARCHITECT
WHO, WHEN HIS ORIGINAL PLAN WAS REJECTED AS
TOO EXPENSIVE, INCORPORATED A MINIATURE OF IT
IN THE FINAL STRUCTURE **AS A CHIMNEY**

FIGURE STONES
NATURAL CHUNKS OF
FLINT SHAPED LIKE
THE HEAD OF
A MONKEY
*WERE VENERATED IN
PREHISTORIC FRANCE*

FREDERICK
AN
HEIR TO
THE THRONE
OF DENMARK
WAS
DECORATED
WITH
HIS
COUNTRY'S
MOST
DISTINGUISHED
AWARD,
*THE ORDER
OF THE
ELEPHANT,*
IN 1753
ON THE
DAY
HE WAS
BORN

THE
**HYPHENATED
BEECHES**
NEAR
WILLERSHAGEN,
IN MECKLENBURG,
GERMANY

THE TUVANS of Siberia RIDE ON THE BACKS OF REINDEER-- AND ALWAYS WHISPER THEIR DESTINATION INTO THE EAR OF THEIR MOUNT

WHAT'S IN A NAME?
XAVIER CHARLES INGRAM (1820-1911) of London, England, WHOSE INITIALS XCI ARE THE ROMAN NUMERALS FOR 91- AND HIS FATHER, WHO HAD THE SAME NAME, BOTH LIVED TO THE AGE OF 91

THE GOLDEN EAGLE NUGGET FOUND IN LARKINVILLE, WESTERN AUSTRALIA, IN 1931, WEIGHED 126 POUNDS AND WAS SOLD FOR $30,000

THE PALACE OF JUSTICE IN BRUSSELS, BELGIUM, IS THE LARGEST STRUCTURE ERECTED ANY-WHERE IN THE WORLD IN THE 19TH CENTURY.
IT HAS AN AREA OF 287,292 SQUARE FEET AND ITS DOME IS 338 FEET HIGH

THE TEMPLE BUILT IN ROME, ITALY, IN 161, BY EMPEROR ANTONINUS PIUS FOR HIS WIFE, FAUSTINA, TODAY HAS INSIDE IT THE CHURCH OF SAN LORENZO de MIRANDA

THE SHIP THAT COULD NOT BE WRECKED!

THE "S.S. VICTORIAN"
200 FEET LONG

CONTINUED 2,000 MILES TO ITS
DESTINATION AFTER HAVING IMPALED
ITSELF ON A JAGGED STONE THAT
PENETRATED 5 FEET ABOVE
THE VESSEL'S LOWER DECK

THE CAPTAIN AND CREW BUILT A
COFFERDAM OUT OF HEAVY TIMBER
FROM THE SHIP'S HOUSING, PUMPED
IT OUT, UNLOADED THE CARGO, WAITED UNTIL
A HIGH WAVE LIFTED THE SHIP OFF THE
ROCK AND THEN REPAIRED THE HULL

THE CONFEDERATE ROSE

HAS BLOOMS
THAT ARE
WHITE IN
THE MORNING
PINK AT
NOON AND
RED IN THE
EVENING

THE FIRST COINS OF A STABLE WEIGHT

WERE GOLD OXHEADS
--MINTED IN CRETE
3400 YEARS AGO
THEY WERE USED
BOTH AS
CURRENCY
AND AS WEIGHTS

ALL SAINTS' CHURCH

in Canberra, Australia,
ORIGINALLY SERVED AS A
RAILROAD STATION IN SYDNEY

THE 787-TON STRUCTURE WAS DISASSEMBLED,
MOVED 200 MILES ON 83 TRAILER TRUCKS,
AND THEN REASSEMBLED WITHOUT LOSS
OF A SINGLE STONE

"HAFFIE"

A CAT OWNED BY
MRS. GLENN MAY, OF
MASSILLON, OHIO,
IS HALF BLACK
AND HALF ORANGE

THE LEAF WORM
IN SHAPE, COLOR AND SHADING *IT RESEMBLES A SMALL GREEN LEAF*

THE **POT-BELLY PALMS**, CUBA, PALMS WHICH, AS THEY GROW OLDER, *GET LARGER AND LARGER POT-BELLIES*

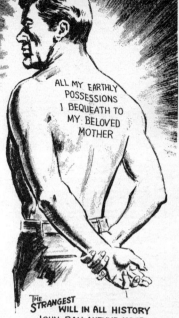

ALL MY EARTHLY POSSESSIONS I BEQUEATH TO MY BELOVED MOTHER

THE **Strangest WILL IN ALL HISTORY**
JOHN BALLANTYNE HOOD WHO DIED IN PITTSBURGH, PA., IN 1917, *HAD HIS WILL TATTOOED ON HIS BACK*
THE WILL WAS DECLARED INVALID BECAUSE IT HAD NOT BEEN LEGALLY WITNESSED

THE **2nd EARL OF LEICESTER OF HOLKHAM**
(1822-1909) SAT IN THE BRITISH HOUSE OF LORDS *FOR 66 YEARS WITHOUT EVER MAKING A SPEECH*

THE MOST AMAZING
MARITAL MATCH
IN ALL HISTORY!

LUZIE RITTENHEIMMAN
(1869-1911)
of Leipzig, Germany,
WAS MARRIED
SUCCESSIVELY
TO FOUR HUSBANDS
WHOSE LAST NAMES WERE
LUZIE--RITTEN--HEIM--MANN!

from an old print

A STONE ISLAND IN THE TIBER RIVER, IN ROME, ITALY,
CARVED INTO THE SHAPE OF A SHIP WHICH
MADE A PILGRIMAGE TO GREECE IN 291 B.C.
*TO BRING BACK A SACRED SERPENT IT WAS BELIEVED
WOULD END AN EPIDEMIC SWEEPING ROME*
THE SERPENT ESCAPED AND SWAM TO THE ROCKY ISLAND
--WHICH THEN BECAME AN OFFICIAL SANCTUARY

A MAP OF THE
WORLD
DESIGNED IN
1530 BY THE
SPANISH
CARTOGRAPHER,
PEDRO APIANO,
REFLECTS THE
PREVAILING BELIEF
THAT THE WORLD
*WAS SHAPED
LIKE A HEART*

PIGEONS
WERE USED IN SIEGES IN THE 15th AND 16th
CENTURIES TO SET FIRE TO WOOD BUILDINGS
AGAINST WHICH THE BIRDS WERE LAUNCHED
WITH TORCHES AFFIXED TO THEIR BODIES

THE **BADGE** OF **OFFICE** OF EVERY CHIEF JUSTICE OF COLONIAL AMERICA'S ADMIRALTY COURT --WHICH TRIED 18TH CENTURY PIRATES-- WAS A PAIR OF SOLID SILVER OARS, EACH TWO FEET LONG

THE ELEPHANT THAT DROVE OFF A BAND OF PIRATES

"ROME" A SAILING SHIP RETURNING FROM SUMATRA WAS SAVED FROM PIRATES OFF MUSCAT, IN THE GULF OF OMAN, WHEN ITS SKIPPER, CAPTAIN SAMUEL KENNEDY, *FREED AN ELEPHANT HE WAS TRANSPORTING ON DECK*

THE SIGHT OF THE STRANGE MONSTER AND ITS TRUMPETINGS TERRIFIED THE ARAB PIRATES AND THEY FLED IN CONFUSION

THE MEMORIAL TO A PEDDLER'S PACK
AN EPITAPH NEAR CLONCURRY, QUEENSLAND, AUSTRALIA, OVER THE SPOT WHERE AN ITINERANT LABORER WHO HAD WON $125,000 IN A LOTTERY BURIED FOREVER HIS PACK --CALLED "MATILDA" IN AUSTRALIAN SLANG

IN MEMORY OF MATILDA

THE WINGLESS CAPE CAVE LOCUST
FOUND ONLY ON CAPE YORK PENINSULA, AUSTRALIA, *HAS ANTENNAE 3 TIMES AS LONG AS ITS BODY*

A
5-FRANC COIN
MINTED BY NAPOLEON I, IN 1805, WAS SHUNNED BY FRENCHMEN BECAUSE OF A RUMOR THAT IT CONTAINED LESS THAN ITS FACE AMOUNT OF SILVER— THE EMPEROR OVERNIGHT MADE IT POPULAR BY ANNOUNCING THAT A CHECK FOR A MILLION FRANCS HAD BEEN SECRETED IN ONE OF THE COINS— *A CHECK THAT HAS NEVER BEEN FOUND TO THIS DAY*

THE CUSTOMS HOUSE
IN BERNE, SWITZERLAND, ORIGINALLY SERVED *AS A CITY GATE*

THE
REV. DR. DAVID CALDWELL
(1725-1824)
OF LANCASTER, PENNSYLVANIA, WHILE A STUDENT AT PRINCETON UNIVERSITY

FOR A PERIOD OF 4 YEARS NEVER ONCE SLEPT IN A BED

DR. CALDWELL WAS FOR 56 YEARS THE PASTOR OF TWO CHURCHES, A PHYSICIAN, AND HEADMASTER OF A BOYS' SCHOOL

COOKING POTS
IN ANCIENT TIMES WERE FASHIONED *FROM THE JOINTS OF PREHISTORIC ANIMALS*

THE BLEEDING TOOTH
A SHELL SO NAMED BECAUSE TEETH APPEAR TO PROTRUDE *FROM A BLEEDING GUM*

PROFESSOR FRANÇOIS de MAIRON (1257-1327) OF THE UNIVERSITY OF PARIS, FRANCE, FOR 15 YEARS LECTURED EVERY WEEKDAY FROM 6 A.M. TO 6 P.M.

A HORNETS' NEST SHAPED LIKE THE *HEAD OF A STEER* Submitted by L.M. La Valley, Bernardston, Mass.

The WATCHTOWER of MAKALLAH in Hadramaut, Arabia, WAS LOCATED NOT ON THE MOST STRATEGIC SITE — BUT ON A HUGE ROCK CARVED BY NATURE IN AN ALMOST PERFECT PROFILE OF THE TOWER'S BUILDER

THE WEATHER-FISH
PREDICTS STORMY WEATHER *BY RACING FORWARD--AND BACKWARD*

THE FANTAIL WARBLER
BUILDS ITS NEST ATOP REEDS *SO ITS BROOD WILL BE GENTLY ROCKED BY THE BREEZES*

COTTON TISSUES EACH 6 INCHES SQUARE, ARE USED ON THE ISLAND OF BUTON, THE SO. CELEBES, INDONESIA, *AS MONEY*

THE SONG THAT SAVED 400 LIVES!

A FORCE OF 400 WELSHMEN
INVADING SAINT MALO, FRANCE, ON SEPT. 6, 1759
SANG AN ANCIENT BRETON SONG AS THEY ADVANCED—
A BRETON ARMY LAY IN AMBUSH, BUT WHEN ITS
SOLDIERS HEARD THE SONG, DATING BACK TO A TIME
WHEN THE WELSH AND BRETONS WERE ONE NATION,
THE DEFENDERS AROSE FROM THEIR CONCEALMENT
AND JOINED IN THE SONG—
BOTH FORCES IGNORED THE ORDERS OF THEIR OFFICERS
AND THE INVADERS REEMBARKED—*WITHOUT EITHER
SIDE HAVING FIRED A SINGLE SHOT!*

THE TEMPLE THAT SERVES AS A LIE DETECTOR
The RUINED TEMPLE OF JETAVANARAMA, Ceylon,
IS REGARDED WITH SUCH REVERENCE
*THAT NATIVES WHOSE TESTIMONY HAS BEEN
QUESTIONED ARE FORCED TO REPEAT THEIR
STATEMENTS IN ITS SHADOWS*

THE DAHLIA ANEMONE
WHICH CONSUMES SMALL CRABS
GETS ITS NAME BECAUSE IT RESEMBLES THE FLOWER
IN BOTH COLOR AND SHAPE

CHINESE JUNKS ACTUALLY ORIGINATED IN INDIA

THE **MAN** WHOSE NAME IS WRITTEN IN THE STARS
GEORG FISCHBERG (1789-1873) A BOOKKEEPER AT THE IMPERIAL ASTRONOMICAL OBSERVATORY, IN VIENNA, AUSTRIA, ON HIS OWN TIME AT NIGHT DISCOVERED 81 NEW STARS —ALL OF WHICH BEAR HIS NAME

THE **GREY CROSS** OF THE **IDAR WOODS** Germany ERECTED IN 1572, MARKS THE SPOT WHERE A JEALOUS YOUNG GERMAN KILLED A GIRL AND HER SWEETHEART, AND UPON RETURNING TO THE SCENE OF THE CRIME WAS *HIMSELF SLAIN THERE BY THE GIRL'S FATHER*

THE **MARQUIS** de **FEUQUIÈRE** (1590-1640) WAS A COLONEL IN THE FRENCH ARMY COLLECTING FULL SALARY *2 WEEKS BEFORE HE WAS BORN* THE MARQUIS, WHO WAS GRANTED THIS DISTINCTION BY KING HENRY IV BECAUSE OF HIS FATHER'S HEROISM, WAS SLAIN IN BATTLE MAY 14, 1640 --50 YEARS TO THE DAY AFTER THE DEATH OF HIS FATHER

AN **IMPRINT** FOUND PRESERVED IN THE CLAY OF GAUBERT CAVE, IN DORDOGNE, FRANCE, IS THAT OF A LEAF OF THE COCCULUS PLANT --USED BY PREHISTORIC CAVEMEN AS A NARCOTIC

ON THIS HIGHWAY THE PEOPLE CARRY THE CARS!

The Chandrigiri Pass LINKING INDIA AND KATMANDU, THE CAPITAL OF NEPAL, IS 8,000 FEET HIGH AND SO TORTUOUS A ROAD THAT AUTOMOBILES SHIPPED FROM INDIA TO NEPAL *ARE CARRIED ON THE BACKS OF AS MANY AS 120 MEN*

THE **PULPIT** OF THE CHURCH OF ST. MARTIN IN BOLSWARD, NETHERLANDS, WAS CARVED FROM A SINGLE BLOCK OF WOOD

QUEEN ELEONORA (1599-1655) WIDOW OF KING GUSTAVUS ADOLPHUS OF SWEDEN, WHO WAS SLAIN IN BATTLE IN 1632, *HAD HER HUSBAND'S HEART EMBALMED AND WORE IT IN A JEWELED LOCKET FOR 23 YEARS*

CAT WITH THE OUTLINE OF A GORILLA ON ITS BACK
Submitted by Mrs. Lesta Spilman Vallejo, Calif.

A STONE SHAPED LIKE A THUMB
Submitted by RAY HALEY Lakewood, Ohio

THE WORST DRESSED BILLIONAIRE IN ALL HISTORY!

CALIPH ABDALLAH MANSUR
(712-775) OF BAGHDAD

DURING HIS ENTIRE REIGN OWNED ONLY 2 GARMENTS --AN OFFICIAL ROBE HE INHERITED FROM HIS BROTHER AND ONE HE PURCHASED SECOND HAND FOR 22 CENTS AND *WORE EVERY DAY FOR 21 YEARS*

HIS TREASURY HELD 140 TONS OF GOLD THE EQUIVALENT TODAY OF $14,000,000,000

THE CATHEDRAL OF EMBRUN WAS BUILT BY KING LOUIS XI OF FRANCE, WHO OBTAINED A PAPAL DECREE GIVING THE RANK OF CHIEF CANON OF THE CATHEDRAL TO EVERY RULER OF THE COUNTRY --AN HONOR NOW BESTOWED ON EACH FRENCH PRESIDENT

NATIVES on the island of Niutao, in the Ellice Islands ONCE WORSHIPED AS DIVINE THE CENTER POST SUPPORTING THE ROOF OF THEIR HOME THEY CONSIDERED IT DIVINE BECAUSE OF ITS CENTRAL POSITION

A JADE BOULDER FOUND BY ERNEST PORTER, NEAR MONTEREY, CALIF., IN 30 FEET OF WATER AND POLISHED BY NATURE *WEIGHS 1,307 POUNDS*

NOW OWNED BY LEROY B. CHILDS, LAGUNA BEACH, CALIF.

SEÑORA SABINA TORRIJOS
(1801-1871) OF TOLEDO, SPAIN,
COULD ONLY READ A BOOK
WHEN ITS LINES WERE REFLECTED BACKWARDS BY A MIRROR
SHE COULD WRITE CORRECTLY WITH HER LEFT HAND AND IN REVERSE WITH HER RIGHT

BRONZE COINS SHAPED LIKE TUNA WERE USED BY ANCIENT GREEKS INHABITING THE BLACK SEA COAST BECAUSE THEIR FIRST CURRENCY *WAS LIVE FISH*

THE INHUMAN PRISON IN WHICH THE CELLS WERE COFFINS!

PRISONERS, in Urga, Mongolia, FOR CENTURIES WERE CONFINED IN PADLOCKED COFFINS WHICH THEY NEVER LEFT -- AND IN WHICH THEY WERE *BURIED WHEN THEY DIED*

THE MOST ASTOUNDING SCHOLAR OF THE SCRIPTURES IN HISTORY

LUIS de PELLETAN (1663-1733) A SPANIARD WHO WAS A LIBRARIAN IN PARIS, FRANCE. COMMITTED TO MEMORY THE ENTIRE CONTENTS OF *THE BIBLE, IN FRENCH, HEBREW AND LATIN, THE KORAN, THE HOLY BOOK OF ISLAM AND THE THERAVADA, THE BUDDHIST SCRIPTURES IN THE ORIGINAL PALI!*

A *MINIATURE VIOLA* CONSTRUCTED OF GUMWOOD AND MAPLE WITH ITS STRINGS CONSISTING OF HUMAN HAIRS AND MEASURING ONLY 9/16 OF AN INCH CARVED BY DAVID W. DUGGER Seattle, Wash.

A SET OF PLAYING CARDS MADE IN INDIA *FROM FISH SCALES -- COATED WITH LACQUER*

ANTONIO LONHOSO (1770-1870)

AND HIS DAUGHTER, LENORA, (1790-1890) BOTH OF OPORTO, PORTUGAL -- EACH WAS BORN ON **MAY 26th** AND EACH DIED ON **MAY 26th** -- *ON THEIR 100th BIRTHDAY*

THE MOST ASTOUNDING ACT OF JUSTICE IN ALL HISTORY!

SULTAN MUHAMMAD bin TUGLUQ

EMPEROR OF INDIA FROM 1325 TO 1351
WITH POWER OF LIFE AND DEATH OVER 100,000,000
SUBJECTS, PERMITTED HIMSELF TO BE HAULED INTO
A LOWLY MAGISTRATE'S COURT ON A 20-YEAR-OLD
YOUTH'S CHARGE THE MONARCH HAD UNJUSTLY
CAUSED HIM TO BE FLOGGED 21 TIMES
FOR FRIGHTENING THE SULTAN'S HORSE

*THE EMPEROR WAS FOUND GUILTY, ORDERED
WHIPPED 21 TIMES BY THE YOUTH -- AND
THE SENTENCE WAS DULY CARRIED OUT!*

NOW AINT
THAT TOO BAD

Epitaph ON THE GRAVE OF CHARLES de PLESSE
WHO DIED IN 1907 AT THE AGE OF 53
Rosehill Cemetery, Chicago, Ill.

THE MOST AMAZING DEMONSTRATION OF REVERENCE IN ALL HISTORY!

ANTONIO COSTA e CANTO
(1822-1882)
of Santarem, Portugal,
REPEATED THE LORD'S
PRAYER FROM MEMORY
EACH DAY FOR 30 YEARS
-- IN 100 LANGUAGES

A TRANSPARENT
GOLDEN COCOON
IS CONSTRUCTED ON A
LEAF BY THE CHRYSALIS
OF THE LANARIA MOTH
of W. Africa, *TO FOOL PREDATORS-*
THE CHRYSALIS HIDES UNDER A
SILKEN BLANKET ON THE SAME LEAF

150

THE ABSENT-MINDED PROFESSOR
Paul Ehrlich
(1854-1915) FAMED NOBEL PRIZE WINNER IN MEDICINE, WAS SO FORGETFUL THAT WHEN A SCIENTIFIC IDEA OCCURRED TO HIM AWAY FROM HIS LABORATORY HE WOULD *MAIL HIMSELF A POSTCARD*

THE CASTLE OF KARLSFRIEDE
in Luckendorf, Czechoslovakia, BUILT TO BAR THE PATH OF AN ENEMY INVASION, WAS CONSTRUCTED IN 1581 BY 583 MEN *IN JUST 9 WEEKS*

THE INSTITUTE OF NATURAL SCIENCE
IN DOBERAN, GERMANY, WAS CONSTRUCTED ENTIRELY BY 20 TEACHERS AND 300 STUDENTS --FROM 120,000 BRICKS MADE BY THE STUDENTS THEMSELVES

THE MAN WHO "ATE HIS NAME" EVERY DAY FOR 60 YEARS!
MICHAEL BREBUMICHE (1840-1918) of Lancaster, England, NEVER VARIED HIS BREAKFAST FOR 21,915 CONSECUTIVE MORNINGS PATTERNING THE MEAL ON HIS SURNAME

BREad   BUtter
MIlk   CHEese

A DECORATIVE STONE IN THE WALL OF A HOME IN RADSTADT, AUSTRIA, ORIGINALLY WAS THE GRAVESTONE FOR A LOST CHILD--*BUT THE YOUNGSTER WAS FOUND UNHARMED*

THE DRONE FLY MIMICS THE HONEYBEE *RESEMBLING IT IN COLOR, SIZE AND ACTIONS*

THE VIVIPAROUS WATER LILY ALWAYS GROWS A NEW PLANT FROM THE CENTER OF ITS LEAF

PORTOVENERE
a town in Italy,
IN 1131 WAS SOLD TO
THE REPUBLIC OF GENOA
FOR 40 CENTS

THE COAT OF ARMS
OF ITALY'S BORGHESE FAMILY
WAS CREATED BY CAMILLO
BORGHESE IN 1605 BECAUSE ON
THE DAY HE BECAME POPE PAUL V
*HE SAW AN EAGLE ALIGHT
ON THE DRAGON IN THE
COAT OF ARMS OF
POPE GREGORY XIII*

WILLIAM I (1797-1888)

KING OF PRUSSIA AND EMPEROR OF GERMANY,
*WAS THE FIRST MONARCH
TO RIDE IN A TRAIN*
HE RODE A GERMAN TRAIN FROM NUREMBERG
TO FÜRTH ON JAN. 12, 1836
--AFTER WAITING UNTIL IT HAD BEEN IN
SERVICE SIX MONTHS TO ASSURE
HIMSELF IT WAS SAFE TRANSPORTATION

A **PEARL** WORTH **$45,000**
WAS GIVEN BY JULIUS CAESAR
TO SERVILIA
*--THE MOTHER OF BRUTUS WHO
LATER MURDERED CAESAR*

THE HOLY VIAL
IN THE TREASURY OF THE CATHEDRAL
OF REIMS, FRANCE, USED TO ANOINT
EVERY FRENCH KING SINCE 496
*STILL CONTAINS SOME OF THE OIL
USED AT THE CORONATION OF
KING CLOVIS 1,476 YEARS AGO*

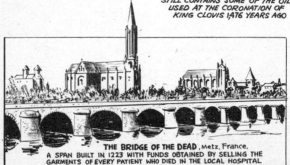

THE BRIDGE OF THE DEAD, Metz, France,
A SPAN BUILT IN 1223 WITH FUNDS OBTAINED BY SELLING THE
GARMENTS OF EVERY PATIENT WHO DIED IN THE LOCAL HOSPITAL

THE TWINS WHOSE NAMES WERE DICTATED BY NATURE!

THE MEUDELLE TWINS
WERE BORN IN PARIS, FRANCE, IN 1901
WITH THE INITIALS OF THE MATERNAL GRANDPARENT
AFTER WHOM EACH WAS NAMED, IN THE FORM
OF BIRTHMARKS ON THEIR SHOULDERS

THE BOY BORE THE INITIALS "T.R." AND
WAS NAMED FOR HIS GRANDFATHER,
THEODORE RODOLPHE

HIS SISTER WAS BORN WITH THE INITIALS
"B.V." AND WAS NAMED FOR HER GRANDMOTHER,
BERTHE-VIOLETTE

THE TWIN CHURCHES OF MILAN - Italy -

THE CHURCH OF SANTA MARIA INCORONATA
ACTUALLY COMPRISES 2 CHURCHES
--ONE BUILT BY DUKE FRANCESCO SFORZA IN 1451,
AND THE OTHER CONSTRUCTED BESIDE IT BY HIS WIFE
AS AN EXPRESSION OF LOVE FOR HER HUSBAND

COPPER ARMBANDS
IN SPIRAL FORM
WHICH UNTIL
RECENT YEARS
DOUBLED AS
ORNAMENTS
AND CURRENCY
IN WEST AFRICA
*VIBRATED LIKE
TUNING FORKS
TO PRODUCE A
CONSTANT TUNE*

THE **GREEN-BILLED CUCKOO**
of Ceylon
IS THE ONLY
TYPE OF CUCKOO
THAT BUILDS ITS
OWN NEST AND
HATCHES ITS
OWN YOUNG

Glückliche Reise

Epitaph ON THE GRAVE
OF HERBERT GÜNTHER, IN
THE CEMETERY OF ENCHENDORF,
BAVARIA,--WISHING HIM
A "HAPPY JOURNEY"

153

THE FORTUNE-TELLER WHO CHANGED THE COURSE OF HISTORY!

MARIE - ANNE LENORMAND (1772-1845)
A CELEBRATED FORTUNE-TELLER, WAS CONSULTED BY AN OFFICER IN THE FRENCH ARMY
--FRUSTRATED IN 1795 BY HIS DIM PROSPECTS FOR PROMOTION--ON WHETHER HE SHOULD
TRANSFER TO THE ARMY OF TURKEY. SHE PERSUADED HIM TO REMAIN A FRENCH
SOLDIER AND PREDICTED HE WOULD RISE TO HIGH RANK

HIS NAME WAS NAPOLEON BONAPARTE!

JAMES COWLEY
(1854-1937)
of Halton Gill,
England,
WAS A PEDDLER
OF TEXTILES
FOR 70 YEARS

PROFESSOR ELLWOOD CUBBERLEY
(1868-1941)
WHO TAUGHT AT
STANFORD UNIVERSITY
FOR 35 YEARS,
DONATED TO THE
SCHOOL UPON HIS
RETIREMENT HIS
*ENTIRE SALARY OF
$168,166.65*
--PLUS MORE THAN
$500,000 HE HAD
EARNED IN THAT
PERIOD BY WISE
INVESTMENTS

THE **WOMAN**
TO WHOM THE
GOOD BOOK WAS
MORE THAN AN
INSPIRATION!
KATHARINE HERBIGER
(1856-1916)
of London, England,
WHO WAS NEARSIGHTED
ALL HER LIFE, COULD
READ ONLY ONE BOOK
WITHOUT GLASSES
-- THE BIBLE!

THE FISHING BOATS
USED BY TIBETANS ON THE TSANGPO RIVER,
EACH CONSISTS OF 4 SMALL WILLOW
FRAME BOATS ENCASED IN LEATHER
--LINKED TOGETHER BY A PLATFORM

**THE HARMLESS PLANT
THAT WAS USED IN
20,000 MURDERS!**

A SPRIG OF PARSLEY
WAS CARRIED IN 1937 BY
EACH DOMINICAN SOLDIER
HUNTING DOWN HAITIANS, AND
ANY PEASANT WHO COULD
NOT CORRECTLY PRONOUNCE
ITS NAME IN SPANISH
WAS SLAIN ON THE SPOT!

20,000 WERE KILLED
BECAUSE THEY REVEALED
THEMSELVES AS HAITIANS
BY REPLYING "PEREGIL"
INSTEAD OF "PEREJIL"

THIS ARCHITECT
IS FOR THE BIRDS
THE NEST
OF THE WHITE-EARED
HUMMINGBIRD, DURING
ITS CONSTRUCTION, IS
ANCHORED TO BRANCHES
BY THE HAIRS OF
GALL NUTS
-- WHICH BREAK
WHEN THE NEST
IS OCCUPIED,
ALLOWING IT TO
SWING FREELY

WOMEN PILGRIMS
ATTENDING A FESTIVAL HELD IN NEPAL
EVERY 12 YEARS WHEN THE PLANET JUPITER
ENTERS THE CONSTELLATION OF AQUARIUS
WEAR DAZZLING COSTUMES OF 1,000 COLORS

THE MOST GENEROUS POETRY PATRON
IN ALL HISTORY !

SULTAN MAHMUD el GHAZNI (967-1030) of India
MAINTAINED AT HIS COURT 8 POETS
*EACH OF WHOM WAS AWARDED HIS WEIGHT IN GOLD
ANNUALLY FOR 30 YEARS*

WOLFFIA ONLY 1/25th OF AN INCH LONG
*IS THE SMALLEST FLOWER PLANT
IN ALL NATURE*

THE STAND IN THE CATHEDRAL OF BARCELONA, SPAIN, FOR THE RECEPTACLE IN WHICH THE CONSECRATED HOST IS DISPLAYED, ORIGINALLY *WAS THE SOLID SILVER THRONE OF KING MARTIN OF ARAGON*

PLENNIE L. WINGO of Los Angeles, Calif., WALKED ACROSS THE U.S. AND EUROPE *BACKWARDS* HE WORE SUNGLASSES EQUIPPED WITH REAR VIEW MIRRORS -- AND IN PITTSBURGH, PA., RECEIVED A TRAFFIC TICKET FOR WALKING BACKWARDS

THE GREEK TEMPLE OF SEGESTA
IN SICILY, STARTED IN 420 B.C.-
BECAUSE ITS CONSTRUCTION WAS
HALTED BY AN ENEMY INVASION
*HAS BEEN LEFT UNFINISHED
FOR NEARLY 2,400 YEARS*

The **PROUD MONARCH WHO
PREFERRED HANDOUTS
TO A PENSION**
KING GUSTAVUS IV (1778-1837)
DEPOSED IN 1809 AFTER
A REIGN OF 17 YEARS,
SPURNED AN OFFICIAL
PENSION EQUIVALENT IN
SPENDING POWER TODAY
TO $720,000 A YEAR
-- EXISTING FOR THE NEXT
28 YEARS ON THE
*CHARITY OF
RELATIVES AND
FRIENDS*

THE
**NO. 1 BUILDER IN
ALL HISTORY**
EMPEROR ASOKA
BUDDHIST RULER OF INDIA
FROM 264 TO 227 B.C.,
CONSTRUCTED 84,000 TEMPLES
-- *EACH DESIGNED TO SHELTER
A SMALL RELIC OF BUDDHA*

**DENISE
JEAN
MATRAW**
OF
WILLISTON,
VERMONT,
WAS
BORN
WITH
4
*FUNCTIONING
KIDNEYS*

EMPEROR FREDERICK II (1194-1250) OF GERMANY, AT THE AGE OF **7** COULD SPEAK ITALIAN, LATIN, ARABIC, GREEK AND HEBREW *--BUT NOT GERMAN*

Submitted by James Belfort, Wellesley, Mass.

WALTER WILLIAMS (1864-1935) JOURNALIST AND EDUCATOR, BECAME PRESIDENT OF THE UNIVERSITY OF MISSOURI *ALTHOUGH HE NEVER ATTENDED COLLEGE-* HIS FORMAL EDUCATION ENDED WHEN HE WAS **13**

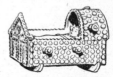

ATTRACTIVE CRADLES WERE PRODUCED BY THE ADAMS FAMILY, OF STOKE-UPON-TRENT, ENGLAND, FOR 100 YEARS ENTIRELY FROM POTTERY

THE **OPOSSUM** BUILDS ITS NEST FROM MATERIALS TRANSPORTED *BY LOOPING ITS TAIL DOWNWARD*

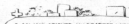

I AM NOT GRIEVED MY DEAREST WIFE
SLEEP ON I'VE GOT ANOTHER WIFE
THEREFORE I CANNOT COME TO THEE
FOR I MUST GO AND LIVE WITH SHEE

EPITAPH IN HEREFORD CHURCHYARD, ENGLAND

The **OLD COVERED BRIDGE**
ON WILLIS CREEK, IN GUERNSEY COUNTY, OHIO,
WAS BUILT IN 1828 OVER DRY LAND -- AND THE
RIVER WAS THEN DIVERTED UNDER IT --
*BECAUSE ITS BUILDERS COULDN'T FIGURE OUT
HOW TO CONSTRUCT IT OVER WATER*

A **ROMAN COIN**
FEATURING
A SPANISH
TEMPLE -
*2 OF THE
SUPPORTING
COLUMNS
REPRESENTED
TUNAS*

A **PETRIFIED
HORSE**
FOUND IN FRANCE
AND NOW IN
A PARIS MUSEUM
*IS AS SMALL
AS A DOG*

The **STRANGEST COINCIDENCE OF
CRIME AND PUNISHMENT
IN ALL HISTORY!**
JEAN-MARIE DUNBARRY
CONVICTED OF MURDERING HIS FATHER,
WAS GUILLOTINED IN PARIS, FRANCE,
AT THE AGE OF 26, ON FEB. 13, 1846.
HIS GREAT-GRANDFATHER, ALSO NAMED
JEAN-MARIE DUNBARRY, AND ALSO
CONVICTED OF KILLING *HIS* FATHER,
*WAS EXECUTED AT THE AGE OF 26
ON FEBRUARY 13, 1746*

THE PATIENT PILGRIMS TO THE LAMASERY OF LABRANG
TIBETANS, VISITING THE SACRED LAMASERY OF LABRANG, (China)
CIRCLING THE ENTIRE MOUNTAIN ON WHICH IT STANDS BY FALLING
FORWARD ON THE GROUND, THEN RISING AND FALLING AGAIN
-- *A PAINFUL JOURNEY THAT REQUIRES 7 DAYS*
THEY WEAR SANDALS ON THEIR HANDS BECAUSE OF THE ROCKY
TRAIL OVER WHICH THEY MUST DRAG THEMSELVES FORWARD

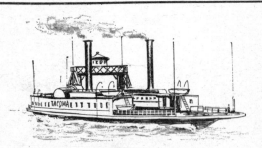

THE *TACOMA* A FERRYBOAT 338 FEET LONG
*WAS BUILT IN NEW YORK CITY, THEN
DISASSEMBLED INTO 57,159 PARTS AND TRANSPORTED
ON ANOTHER SHIP TO PORTLAND, OREGON --*
REASSEMBLED AND LAUNCHED ON MAY 17, 1883,
IT WAS USED FOR YEARS TO TRANSPORT NORTHERN
PACIFIC TRAINS ACROSS THE COLUMBIA RIVER.

THE AMAZING MISS MARIA!

MARIA THERESIA PARADIES (1759-1824) THE CELEBRATED AUSTRIAN PIANIST WHO WAS BLIND FROM THE AGE OF 5, COULD PLAY A PIANO RECITAL, ENGAGE IN A GAME OF CHESS AND SOLVE AN INVOLVED MATHEMATICAL PROBLEM *SIMULTANEOUSLY*

THE HAMMERHEAD OYSTER

FOUND IN TORRES STRAIT, OFF THURSDAY ISLAND, AUSTRALIA, IS SO NAMED BECAUSE ITS SHELL LOOKS LIKE THE HEAD OF A HAMMERHEAD SHARK

EVERY MEMBER

OF THE NISTINARES FAMILY, IN MACEDONIA, ANNUALLY CELEBRATES THE FEAST OF ST. CONSTANTINE AND ST. HELENA BY WALKING AND DANCING ON FIRE *BAREFOOTED —* NONE IS EVER HARMED

THE CHURCH OF BARBOTAN, France,
IS ALSO THE PRINCIPAL GATEWAY TO THE TOWN OF BARBOTAN

THE UMBRELLA BIRD of South America INFLATES ITS CREST OF LONG FEATHERS SO THAT THEY SHIELD ITS HEAD LIKE A *FRINGED SUN SHADE*

THE **CHURCH of DENSUS**, Rumania,
WAS BUILT FROM THE STONES OF A
ROMAN FORTRESS THAT HAD BEEN RAZED
*1,100 YEARS BEFORE CONSTRUCTION
OF THE CHURCH*

DR.
J.I. GUILLOTIN
(1738-1814)
WHO INTRODUCED THE
GUILLOTINE TO FRANCE.
WAS A PREMATURE BABY
-- BORN ON MAY 28,1738,
WHEN HIS MOTHER
BECAME REVOLTED AT
*THE SIGHT OF AN
EXECUTION*

THE**RAFT SNAIL**
(Janthina nitens)
FLOATS BESIDE A
RAFT OF BUBBLES
WHICH IT CREATES
FROM FOAM AND AIR

THE LIBERTY BELL STAMP
FIRST ISSUED IN W. BERLIN, GERMANY, IN 1951, WAS WITHDRAWN
BECAUSE THE CLAPPER WAS ON THE LEFT SIDE OF THE BELL.
REISSUED IN 1952, IT WAS AGAIN WITHDRAWN BECAUSE THE
CLAPPER WAS ON THE RIGHT SIDE -- BUT A THIRD ISSUE WAS
APPROVED WHEN THE CLAPPER WAS CENTERED
TO SIGNIFY NEUTRALITY

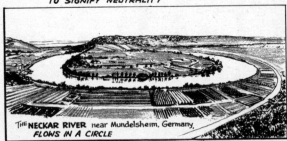

THE**NECKAR RIVER** near Mundelsheim, Germany,
FLOWS IN A CIRCLE

THE **OWL CUP**
of Ochsenfurt,
Germany,
A CUP
THAT HOLDS
3⅓ QUARTS
OF WINE,
HAD TO BE
DRAINED BY
EACH NEW
PROSPECTIVE
MEMBER OF
THE OWL
CLUB IN A
SINGLE DRAFT

THE AMAZING SANTANGELO SUCCESSIONS

FELICE SANTANGELO
(1854-1899) of Rome, Italy,
WAS AN ONLY CHILD
BORN ON THE 17th ANNIVERSARY OF HIS PARENTS' MARRIAGE

HE HAD ONE CHILD, ANGELO,
WHO WAS BORN IN 1891
ON THE 17th ANNIVERSARY OF HIS PARENTS' MARRIAGE

THERE WAS ONE GRANDCHILD,
GIOVANNI, WHO WAS BORN IN 1929
ON THE 17th ANNIVERSARY OF HIS PARENTS' MARRIAGE

THE **KASUGA SHRINE**
OF NARA, JAPAN,
ORIGINALLY CONSTRUCTED IN 768
HAS BEEN DEMOLISHED AND REBUILT
59 TIMES

THE **DEEP-SEA CUTTLEFISH**
HAS DISTRIBUTED THROUGHOUT ITS BODY NUMEROUS LIGHTS THAT SHIMMER IN *CHANGING COLORS*

THE MOST DIFFICULT RIVER CROSSING IN THE WORLD!

A TIBETAN HORSEMAN
TO CROSS THE DZA CHU RIVER IN THE TIBETAN HIGHLANDS
TRUSSES HIS HORSE BY A SLING TO THE ROPE "BRIDGE"
-- AND THEN MUST PULL HIMSELF AND
HIS MOUNT FROM CLIFF TO CLIFF

THE OLDEST CHRISTIAN STRUCTURE IN FRANCE
Le Baptistère St. Jean
in Poitiers, France,
ERECTED IN THE YEAR 320
FOR BAPTISMS BY IMMERSION

THE LILY-LEAF CATERPILLAR
MAKES A CLOAK FOR ITSELF
BY BITING OFF 2 PIECES
OF A LILY PAD AND
*STITCHING THEM AROUND
ITS BODY WITH STRANDS OF
SILK*

**THE MONSTER
of LAKE THINGVALLA**
Iceland
NATURAL FORMATION CREATED BY
LAVA FROM A NEARBY VOLCANO

THE BRAZILIAN WAX PALM
*PROVIDES WOOD FOR BUILDING HOMES
LEAVES FOR THEIR ROOFS
FRUIT TO FEED CATTLE AND
KERNELS TO BREW A SUBSTITUTE FOR COFFEE*

MA IN
VIETNAMESE
MEANS
*BUT, YOUNG,
RICE, HORSE,
GHOST, TOMB
OR MOTHER
-- DEPENDING ON
THE INTONATION*

THE **MARINER** WHO WAS THE FIRST TO READ THE
ANNOUNCEMENT OF HIS OWN BIRTH!
CAPTAIN DANIEL SAUNDERS of the S.S. "KING FREDERICK VII"
OUTWARD BOUND FROM BELFAST, IRE., ON SEPT. 1, 1912, FISHED FROM THE SEA A
BOTTLE CONTAINING A MESSAGE DATED SEPT. 1, 1872, ASKING THE FINDER TO
NOTIFY THE BELFAST FAMILY OF THE CAPTAIN OF THE "MORNING STAR" THAT
HIS WIFE HAD THAT DAY GIVEN BIRTH TO A BABY BOY
CAPTAIN DANIEL SAUNDERS WAS THAT "BABY" -- *THE FIRST PERSON
TO READ OF HIS OWN BIRTH EXACTLY FORTY YEARS BEFORE*

THE TOWERS OF STIRLING CASTLE, IN SCOTLAND, PROVIDE A VIEW OF *12 HISTORIC BATTLEFIELDS AND 12 SCOTTISH COUNTIES*

LOT M. MORRILL (1813-1883) WHO LATER BECAME GOVERNOR OF MAINE, WAS A SCHOOLTEACHER *AT THE AGE OF 16 AND A PRINCIPAL AT 20*

IMAGE BREAD BAKED ANNUALLY IN AUSTRIA ON ST. NICHOLAS DAY *IN THE SHAPE OF VARIOUS ANIMALS*

THE **RYO YEI MARU** A JAPANESE FISHING BOAT, LEFT THE HARBOR OF MISAKI ON DEC.5,1926 WITH A CREW OF 12, *WAS FOUND DRIFTING HELPLESSLY 325 DAYS LATER AND 5,000 MILES OFF HER COURSE-* ABOARD WERE ONLY THE BLEACHED SKELETONS OF 8 MEN AND 2 MUMMIFIED BODIES

THE **BETROTHAL RING** OF THE VIRGIN MARY IS EXHIBITED IN THE CATHEDRAL OF PERUGIA, ITALY, FOR VIEW BY PILGRIMS ONLY **4 DAYS EACH YEAR**

THE **MOTTO** ON THE COAT OF ARMS OF TANANARIVE, MADAGASCAR --A MESSAGE OF HOPE FOR A LAND ONCE SCOURGED BY EPIDEMICS-- READS:
"When a town has 1,000 people, all of them do not die in one day"

AARON BURR (1756-1836) A VICE-PRESIDENT OF THE U.S. AND THE MAN WHO KILLED ALEXANDER HAMILTON IN A DUEL, WAS DIVORCED BY HIS SECOND WIFE, MADAME JUMEL, *ON THE DAY OF HIS DEATH*

THE MOST AMAZING INVALID IN ALL HISTORY!
J.G. EWERT of Hillsboro, Kansas,
WAS CONFINED TO A BED FOR 26 YEARS AND HAD TO BE FED THROUGH A GLASS TUBE BECAUSE HE COULD NOT MOVE HIS JAWS-- YET *HE TAUGHT FRENCH, LATIN, GREEK, HEBREW AND DUTCH, WAS ACTIVE IN WAR RELIEF WORK, SERVED AS AN EDITOR AND WRITER AND DID HIS OWN TYPING ALTHOUGH A BROTHER HAD TO HELP HIM SHIFT BACK THE CARRIAGE AT THE END OF EACH LINE*

A **RESTAURANT**
IN DUERKHEIM, IN THE GERMAN PALATINATE
--*LOCATED IN AN ACTUAL WINE CASK*

THE **OLDEST KNOWN SAMPLE CASE**
OF A TRAVELING SALESMAN
EXCAVATED IN KOPPENOW,
POMERANIA, GERMANY,
WAS USED TO DISPLAY
BRONZE KNIVES, AXE HEADS,
SWORDS AND JEWELRY
3,000 YEARS AGO

**4 POUNDS
OF BUTTER**
DONATED TO
AN AUCTION
HELD TO FINANCE
CONSTRUCTION OF
COLORADO COLLEGE
*WAS RESOLD
SEVERAL TIMES
AND FINALLY
WENT FOR $180*
(1874)

LUISA ADAMS
(1775- 1852) THE WIFE OF
PRESIDENT JOHN QUINCY ADAMS
IS THE ONLY FIRST LADY OF THE U.S. WHO
WAS BORN IN A FOREIGN COUNTRY
SHE WAS BORN IN LONDON, ENGLAND

THE PADDLE STEAMER THAT MADE ITS MOST MEMORABLE JOURNEY--ON LAND!

THE "TICONDEROGA"
A LAKE CHAMPLAIN STEAMER
220 FEET LONG AND WEIGHING 892 TONS,
TO REACH THE MUSEUM IN SHELBURNE, VT., IN 1955
MADE A 2-MILE OVERLAND JOURNEY
ON ROLLERS-- *THAT TOOK*
65 DAYS, 20 HOURS AND 28 MINUTES

LANDON CARTER HAYNES
WAS A PROFESSOR
AND DEPARTMENT HEAD
AT TUSCULUM COLLEGE,
NEAR GREENEVILLE, TENN.,
FROM 1877 UNTIL 1942,
A PERIOD OF 65 YEARS
Submitted by
MRS. FEROL FROST HUBBS
Greeneville, Tenn.

THE HUGE WEBS
CONSTRUCTED BY
AFRICAN SPIDERS
HANG LIKE BLANKETS
WITH THEIR CORNERS
ATTACHED TO 4 TREES
FORMING AN
IMPENETRABLE MAZE

THE FEMALE GIANT WATERBUG
AFTER LAYING HER EGGS INTIMIDATES
THE FIRST PASSING MALE OF HER SPECIES
*AND FORCES HIM TO CARRY HER EGGS ON
HIS BACK UNTIL THEY HATCH 30 DAYS LATER*
THE FEMALE IS 5 TIMES
AS LARGE AS THE MALE

THE FIRST VIOLIN
WAS CONSTRUCTED
BY PELEGRINO
MICHELI IN
MONTICHIARI,
Italy,
IN 1552
*AND IS
STILL IN
EXISTENCE*

HERE LIES GOTTLIEB MERKEL
WHO IN YOUTH WAS A YOUNG PIG
IN HIS OLD AGE HE BECAME A SWINE
I WONDER WHAT HE MIGHT
BE AT PRESENT

EPITAPH OF AUTHOR G.H. MERKEL
(1769-1850) Doberan, Germany

**IT WASN'T HOW THEY PLAYED THIS GAME
--IT WAS WHETHER THEY WON OR LOST!**
THE *AZTECS* OF ANCIENT MEXICO
PLAYED A GAME RESEMBLING BASKETBALL, BUT
THE CAPTAIN OF THE LOSING TEAM WAS SLAIN AS A SACRIFICE
--WHILE THE WINNING PLAYERS HAD THE RIGHT TO
STRIP THE CLOTHING FROM ANY SPECTATORS THEY COULD CATCH

THE
**WHITE
PELICAN**
IS KEPT AFLOAT
IN THE WATER BY
*A BUILT-IN
PNEUMATIC
LIFE PRESERVER*

A LARGE POCKET
UNDER ITS SKIN IS
INFLATED WITH AIR
DRAWN IN THROUGH
OPENINGS AT THE
ROOTS OF ITS
FEATHERS

THE
SHELL of the HAWKSBILL TURTLE
WAS USED BY THE ANCIENT ROMANS
AS A SHIELD IN BATTLE
*AND AS A BATHTUB AND CRADLE
FOR THEIR CHILDREN*

LAMPROTOXUS
A DEEP-SEA FISH
FOUND OFF IRELAND
HAS SEVERAL ROWS OF
LUMINOUS "PORTHOLES"
*AND AN ANTENNA 5 TIMES
AS LONG AS ITS BODY*

HOVER FLIES
COURT BY *BUTTING HEADS*

JOHANN CHRISTIAN SENCKENBERG (1707-1772)
FOUNDER OF THE ANATOMICAL
INSTITUTE AT THE UNIVERSITY
OF FRANKFURT ON THE MAIN,
GERMANY,
*WAS THE FIRST MAN WHOSE
BODY WAS AUTOPSIED THERE*

THE LIGHTHOUSE
of Westkapelle, Netherlands,
IS A CONVERTED CHURCH TOWER

THE REMAINDER OF THE
CHURCH, WHICH WAS BUILT
IN THE 15th CENTURY, WAS
DESTROYED BY FIRE IN 1831

THE ORIENTAL SHAWL
Yallingup Cave, Australia,
A FANTASTIC DESIGN,
COMPLETE EVEN TO THE
FRINGES, CREATED OF
CALCIUM CARBONATE AND
WATER BY NATURE

BURIAL URNS
ARE USED BY THE MUKULEHE TRIBESMEN OF THE CAMEROONS, AND TWINS ARE BURIED IN URNS WITH 2 SPOUTS --SO EACH SOUL WILL HAVE ITS OWN MEANS OF EXIT

WILLIAM TELL'S FEAT
SHOOTING AN APPLE OFF HIS SON'S HEAD, IS REPEATED EVERY SUMMER SUNDAY IN SWITZERLAND, WITH ACTORS IN INTERLAKEN AND ALTDORF USING ANCIENT CROSSBOWS *TO SHOOT AN APPLE FROM A YOUTH'S HEAD*

THE OFFICIAL EMBLEM
of Penzance, England, BECAUSE THE CITY'S NAME MEANS "HOLY HEAD" IN BRYTHONIC THE LANGUAGE OF ANCIENT BRITAIN, FEATURES *THE HEAD OF ST. JOHN THE BAPTIST ON A SERVING DISH*

ATOMIC BOMB BLAST
NATURAL SANDSTONE FORMATION ON A BOULDER FOUND NEAR KANAB, UTAH
Submitted by Henry Meywes, Albuquerque, N.M.

STOVES
ARE MADE BY NATIVES IN KENYA *FROM THE FEET OF ELEPHANTS*

THE STRANGEST SPEED RECORD IN HISTORY!
GORDON CRAIG
TO TOP A FEAT PERFORMED IN 1890
CLIMBED SUTHERLAND FALLS,
IN NEW ZEALAND, 1,904 FEET HIGH
IN 6 HOURS
--AND THEN DESCENDED AGAIN
THROUGH THE TORRENT OF WATER
DEC. 30, 1950

EMPEROR SHIH HUANG TI
WHO RULED CHINA
FROM 246 TO 210 B.C.,
GAVE 14 OF HIS 25
SONS SURNAMES
FROM WHICH ALL
CHINESE SURNAMES
SINCE HAVE BEEN
ADAPTED

AN **IRON CHEST**
LEFT AT THE BOTTOM OF A WELL WHEN A
ROMAN GARRISON ABANDONED KEMPTEN,
GERMANY, IN 335, YIELDED ENOUGH
TREASURE TO CONSTRUCT 4 CHURCHES
AND THE BELFRY OF ANOTHER (860)

CLAY POTS
BEFORE THE
INVENTION OF
THE POTTER'S
WHEEL, WERE
MADE BY
MIXING CLAY
WITH ASHES,
ROLLING IT INTO
STRIPS, AND THEN
COILING THE
STRIPS INTO THE
SHAPE OF A POT

Jonathan Tate,
Died 1763, age 14,
Effected by inoculation
The means employed his life to save
Hurried him headlong to the grave

Epitaph IN NORTH CEMETERY, VERNON, VT.

THE **CRAPPIE** HAS **50** NAMES —MORE THAN ANY OTHER FISH

THE **HARVEST MOUSE** IS THE ONLY EUROPEAN MAMMAL THAT CAN GRIP WITH ITS TAIL

STATE OF OKLAHOMA
TEXAS COUNTY, ss.

IN THE DISTRICT COURT

Manda Walters, Plaintiff
vs.
J. A. Walters, Defendant

NO. 5060
PETITION

Come now the plaintiff herein named
And for cause of action she's not ashamed
In Texas County she's lived for years
Where joy and happiness has mingled with tears.

A POETIC PLEA
A *DIVORCE SUIT* FILED IN DISTRICT COURT IN GUYMON, OKLA., BY ATTORNEY WALLACE G. HUGHES, *WAS ENTIRELY IN RHYME* (1931)

THE **HORSE THAT LIVED FOR HOURS UNDER THE ICE OF A FROZEN RIVER** FERDINAND von WRANGEL, LEADING A RUSSIAN EXPEDITION TO SIBERIA IN 1821, *SAW HIS HORSE PLUNGE THROUGH THE ICE ON THE DOGDO RIVER*— SEVERAL HOURS LATER NATIVES USING LONG POLES RESCUED THE ANIMAL — *WHICH WAS UNHARMED BY ITS EXPERIENCE* WHEN THE DOGDO AND SOME OTHER SMALL SIBERIAN RIVERS FREEZE OVER, THE WATER BENEATH THE ICE LOWERS SO FAR THAT THE HORSE COULD BREATHE — AND WAS NOT UNDULY CHILLED

EPITAPH OF A WOMAN
*BORN ON A DATE
THAT NEVER WAS!*
St. Peter's Churchyard
Lewes, Delaware

MYSTERIOUS EPITAPH
IN THE OLD BUFFALO
CEMETERY, NEAR
GREENSBORO, N.C.

THE AMAZING MEMORIAL TO A MYTHOLOGICAL LEGEND
A HUGE ARTIFICIAL WATERFALL
CREATED AT THE ROYAL PALACE OF CASERTA, IN ITALY, TO REPRODUCE
THE DEATH OF ACTAEON, THE GREEK HUNTER, WHO AS PUNISHMENT
FOR PEEPING AT THE GODDESS DIANA IN HER BATH, *WAS
CHANGED INTO A STAG AND SLAIN BY HIS OWN DOGS*

THE FIRST STARS AND STRIPES
A FLAG WITH 13 RED AND WHITE
STRIPES AND A FIELD OF STARS
WAS CREATED BY CAPTAIN JOHN
HULBERT, COMMANDING THE THIRD
N.Y. REGIMENT AT FORT TICONDEROGA,
*A YEAR BEFORE BETSY
ROSS MADE HER FLAG*

**FLOATING
COFFEEHOUSE**
ON THE THAMES
RIVER, LONDON,
ENGLAND,
IN THE 18th
CENTURY

THE **COCK of the ROCK** CANNOT SING OR EVEN CHIRP *BUT IT IS THE MOST BEAUTIFUL BIRD IN ALL NATURE*

AGRIMONY AN HERB STILL USED IN MEDICINE WAS BELIEVED BY THE ANCIENT GREEKS *TO HAVE THE POWER TO CURE CATARACTS*

JEAN de HOUSSAYE (1539-1609) of Mt. Valerien, France, ATE ONLY ONE MEAL A DAY --ALWAYS WATER, BREAD AND RAW ROOTS-- *FOR 46 YEARS*

THE **CRIME THAT WAS SOLVED AFTER A 20-YEAR SEARCH BY A BLIND MAN!**
ROBERT ADAM, a baker in Johannesburg, So. Africa, *WAS BLINDED IN 1892 BY A ROBBER TO PREVENT HIM FROM EVER IDENTIFYING HIS ASSAILANT.*
IN 1912 ADAM, GIVEN A USED JACKET, REALIZED IT HAD BEEN WORN BY THE THIEF AT THE TIME OF THE ASSAULT.
ITS ORIGINAL OWNER, A RICHARD SHANGAAN, WAS TRACED, TRIED AND CONVICTED--*BECAUSE ADAM HAD REMEMBERED THE FEEL AND LEATHERY SMELL OF THE ROBBER'S JACKET*

THE MOST FANATICAL CHESS PLAYER IN ALL HISTORY!

MURAR RAO

COMMANDER OF THE MAHRATTA ARMIES OF INDIA FROM 1740 TO 1763 TOOK THOUSANDS OF PRISONERS OF WAR IN HIS CAMPAIGNS AND **PLAYED A GAME OF CHESS WITH EACH PRISONER**

IF THE CAPTIVE WON HE WAS SET FREE -- BUT IF HE LOST HE WAS HURLED TO HIS DEATH FROM THE BATTLEMENTS OF THE FORTRESS!

THE SACRED COMB IS A FISH FOUND ONLY IN LAKE TIBERIAS, IN THE HOLY LAND *-- AND NOWHERE ELSE IN THE WORLD*

MODEL FRIGATE
MADE BY FRENCH PRISONERS AT DARTMOOR PRISON *OUT OF BEEF BONES AND HUMAN HAIR*

THE EARL OF WESTMORLAND
(1759-1841)
LORD LIEUTENANT OF IRELAND FROM 1790 TO 1795, WAS NICKNAMED "EIGHTEEN PENCE" BY THE IRISH BECAUSE A SHILLING, WORTH 12 PENCE, IS TWICE THE SIZE OF A 6-PENCE PIECE --AND WESTMORLAND'S RIGHT EYE WAS EXACTLY TWICE THE SIZE OF HIS LEFT

THE CASTLE OF BOYDAN
IN FRANCE
CONSTRUCTED IN THE 15th CENTURY *WAS CARVED OUT OF A CLIFF OF SOLID ROCK*

The **PALÆOLOGOS PALACE** in Mistra, Greece, NOW A RUIN, STILL HAS CONCEALED IN ITS WALLS THE PIPES OF A CENTRAL HEATING SYSTEM *INSTALLED 800 YEARS AGO* - THE PIPES CIRCULATED BOILING WATER TO HEAT THE ENORMOUS BANQUET HALL OF THE PALACE

THE FEMALE WATER SPIDER
LIVES IN A HOLLOW, BELL-SHAPED UNDER-WATER NEST WHICH SHE STOCKS WITH AIR BY BRINGING IT DOWN *IN BIG BUBBLES FROM THE SURFACE*

TWIN CARROTS SHAPED LIKE A *HUMAN TORSO*

Grown and submitted by MRS. CECILE VACHON Ware, Mass.

BUKURJU
A TUBER CONSIDERED A CURE-ALL BY CHINESE MEDICINE MEN REQUIRES **12** YEARS TO REACH FULL GROWTH AND DEVELOPS ONLY ON THE ROOTS OF *DEAD AKAMATSU TREES*

THE DRINKING CUP USED FOR CENTURIES BY THE SHOEMAKERS' GUILD OF Salisbury, England, *WAS SHAPED LIKE A SHOE*

A MEMORIAL TO
ENRICO TODI
—SLAIN IN THE BATTLE OF MONFALCONE IN 1916—
WHO HAD BEEN ACCEPTED AS A VOLUNTEER IN THE ITALIAN ARMY IN WORLD WAR I
ALTHOUGH HE HAD ONLY ONE LEG AND MARCHED ON CRUTCHES!

BUKUR
A GYPSY OF FELSENDORF, TRANSYLVANIA, WAS SO OVERJOYED AT THE BIRTH OF TWINS THAT HE PLACED THE NEWBORN INFANTS IN A 40-QUART POT AND DANCED FOR A FULL HOUR--*WITH THE POT AND BABIES BALANCED ON HIS HEAD*

HAUSTORIUS
A SAND-BURROWING AMPHIPOD *ALWAYS SWIMS UPSIDE DOWN*

John Hancock

FIRST SIGNER OF THE
DECLARATION OF INDEPENDENCE,
WAS THE ONLY ONE OF THE
SIGNERS WHO HAD ATTENDED
THE CORONATION OF
KING GEORGE III
*WHOM THE DECLARATION
DENOUNCED*

THE **MIGHTY MITE**
Bertholde
A 2½-FOOT
MIDGET, WAS
PRIME MINISTER
OF LOMBARDY
FROM 566 TO 573
—*NEXT TO KING ALBOIN
THE MIGHTIEST MAN
IN THE KINGDOM*

A WASP SKYSCRAPER
CONSTRUCTED BY A COLONY OF BRAZILIAN WASPS
40-STORIES HIGH

THE MAN WHOSE LIFE WAS SAVED BY A GHOULISH JEST!

Sir Hugh Acland of Killerton, England, WAS PRONOUNCED DEAD IN 1770, BUT WAS REVIVED WHEN A FOOTMAN SITTING WITH THE "BODY" POURED A DRINK OF BRANDY DOWN THE "CORPSE'S" THROAT HE LIVED ANOTHER 18 YEARS

THE MAN-EATING LEOPARD OF RUDRAPRAYAG India

A SINGLE LEOPARD THAT IN THE PERIOD FROM JUNE 9, 1918 TO APRIL 14, 1926 **ATE 125 HUMAN BEINGS**

MECHANICAL SINGING BIRD

CONSTRUCTED BY AN EGYPTIAN INVENTOR NAMED HERO **2,000 YEARS AGO** THE BIRD SITS ON AN AIRTIGHT TANK AND SINGS WHEN WATER IS POURED INTO THE TANK THROUGH A FUNNEL VALVE

HOG COINS

MADE IN BERMUDA FROM 1616 TO 1624 *WERE THE FIRST COINS MINTED IN NORTH AMERICA*

MERCHANTS ENTERING THE CITY OF ISTANBUL, TURKEY, FOR CENTURIES BELIEVED THEY WOULD PROSPER ONLY IF THEY *DANCED IN A CIRCLE OUTSIDE THE GATE OF FELICITY--AND THEN PASSED THROUGH IT IN TWO COLUMNS*

THE **HOOPSKIRT** THAT SAVED A MAN'S LIFE!

THE DUKE OF MONTMORENCY PURSUED BY 5 THUGS IN BÉZIERS, FRANCE, IN 1582, ESCAPED THEM WHEN LOUISE de MONTAYNARD HID HIM BENEATH HER HOOPSKIRT *--WHICH MEASURED 12 FEET IN CIRCUMFERENCE*

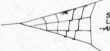

THE **TRIANGLE SPIDER** SPINS A TRIANGULAR SHAPED NET BUT LEAVES ONE MAIN THREAD UNATTACHED *-AND WHEN AN INSECT ENTERS THE WEB THE SPIDER ENTRAPS IT LIKE A FISHERMAN CASTING A NET*

LUCERAM A VILLAGE ON THE FRENCH RIVIERA, WITH A POPULATION OF 1,098 *WAS AN INDEPENDENT REPUBLIC FOR 588 YEARS*

SILVER FOR A BRIEF PERIOD IN 1848 WAS MORE VALUABLE THAN **GOLD** WHEN GOLD WAS FIRST DISCOVERED IN CALIFORNIA 5 SILVER DOLLARS WERE WORTH MORE IN THE U.S. THAN A 5-DOLLAR GOLD PIECE

THE **OLDEST KNOWN "MAGNIFYING GLASS"**

A MAGNIFIER MADE OF GROUND ROCK CRYSTAL FOUND IN THE RUINS OF NINEVEH IN ASSYRIA *AND PROBABLY USED AS AN EYEGLASS BY AN ASSYRIAN KING 2,600 YEARS AGO*

READER IF OF CASH YOU ARE IN WANT OF ANY DIG 10 FEET DEEP AND YOU'LL FIND A PENNY

EPITAPH IN CARLISLE CATHEDRAL CHURCHYARD, ENGLAND *OVER THE GRAVE OF JOHN PENNY*

THE OPERA HOUSE THAT WAS EXECUTED FOR MURDER !

THE PARIS OPERA HOUSE, OUTSIDE WHICH THE DUKE OF BERRY WAS ASSASSINATED AS HE WAS LEAVING THE STRUCTURE ON FEBRUARY 13, 1820, *WAS PUNISHED FOR THE CRIME BY DEMOLITION --AND ITS SITE WAS CONVERTED INTO A PUBLIC PARK*

AN **ARROW** FIRED BY AN ARCHER NAMED ASTOR FROM
THE BESIEGED CITY OF METHONE, GREECE, IN 352 B.C.
HAD ATTACHED TO IT A NOTE WHICH READ:
"ASTOR TO PHILIP'S RIGHT EYE"
THE ARROW STRUCK KING PHILIP II OF MACEDONIA
--DESTROYING HIS RIGHT EYE !

THE NILE STEAMER IN Egypt
ACTUALLY IS 3 SHIPS LASHED TOGETHER
THE LARGEST VESSEL IN THE CENTER CARRIES FIRST-CLASS
PASSENGERS, ANOTHER IS FOR SECOND-CLASS TRAVELERS, AND
THE SMALLEST REPRESENTS THIRD-CLASS TRANSPORTATION

THE **TEMPLE TOWER OF KHAJRAHO**
in India
IS ADORNED BY SCORES OF
MINIATURE REPLICAS OF THE TOWER
--EVIDENCE THAT IT IS ONE OF THE FEW
TEMPLES CONSTRUCTED FROM
A PLANNED DESIGN

THE
**MOST LOYAL
DIPLOMAT**
IN ALL
HISTORY!

SONKOSI

WHILE UNDER
SENTENCE OF
DEATH BY
HIS ZULU KING
PANDA, WAS
DISPATCHED
ON A VITAL
DIPLOMATIC
MISSION
TO NATAL

*—YET HE
PERFORMED HIS
ASSIGNMENT AND
RETURNED HOME
TO KEEP HIS
APPOINTMENT
WITH THE
EXECUTIONER!*
(1855)

**ALFRED
ILG**

(1854-1916)
A SWISS
ENGINEER
SERVED
FOR 10
YEARS AS
*SECRETARY
OF STATE
OF ETHIOPIA*

JOHANNES BUXTORF (1565-1630)
PROFESSOR OF HEBREW AT THE
UNIVERSITY OF BASLE, SWITZERLAND,
FOR 40 YEARS, WAS SUCCEEDED IN
THAT POST BY HIS SON, HIS GRAND-
SON AND HIS GREAT-GRANDSON
-- *THE CHAIR OF HEBREW AT
THE UNIVERSITY BEING FILLED BY
A MEMBER OF THE SAME FAMILY
FOR 142 SUCCESSIVE YEARS*

HIRAM TUTHILL
(1801-1848)
OF WADING RIVER, N.Y.,
SUCCESSIVELY MARRIED
5 MEMBERS OF
THE SAME FAMILY--
3 SISTERS AND
THEIR 2 COUSINS--
ALL NAMED DAVIS

THE
**CHAMELEON
FISH**
THE PIUTE
TROUT of
California
*CHANGES ITS
COLORING
CONSTANTLY*

THE
**REV.
GEORGE
M.TRUNK**
CELEBRATES
MASS IN THE
SLOVENIAN
CATHOLIC
CHURCH, IN
SAN FRANCISCO,
AT 5:45 A.M.
EVERY DAY
*AT THE
AGE OF*
101

A **BOWIE KNIFE** 7 FEET LONG, WHICH WAS HUNG OVER THE CHICAGO PLATFORM
ON WHICH LINCOLN WAS NOMINATED FOR PRESIDENT IN 1860
ENDED DUELING IN AMERICA BY RIDICULE
THE KNIFE WAS A TRIBUTE TO REP. JOHN F. POTTER, OF WISC., A DELEGATE
TO THE REPUBLICAN CONVENTION, WHO ACCEPTED A DUELING CHALLENGE BY
INSISTING THAT IT BE FOUGHT WITH BOWIE KNIVES IN A LOCKED ROOM

BEER MUGS IN ANCIENT ROME WERE OFTEN RING-SHAPED --IN THE BELIEF THAT CIRCULATING THE BEER IMPROVED ITS FLAVOR

© King Features Syndicate 1972. World rights res

LACÉPÈDE

(1756-1825), THE FAMED FRENCH NATURALIST AND COMPOSER, FOR 54 YEARS OF HIS LIFE ATE ONLY ONE MEAL A DAY AND SLEPT ONLY **2 HOURS IN EACH 24** --YET *ENJOYED PERFECT HEALTH*

THE NEST OF THE INDIAN SPARROW IS BOTTLE-SHAPED, PERCHED IN THE HIGHEST AVAILABLE TREE --AND ILLUMINATED BY IMPRISONING FIREFLIES IN MOIST CLAY

2-6

THE **GOOSE FISH** IS SO NAMED BECAUSE ITS FAVORITE FOOD IS THE *GOOSE*

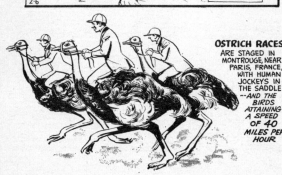

OSTRICH RACES ARE STAGED IN MONTROUGE, NEAR PARIS, FRANCE, WITH HUMAN JOCKEYS IN THE SADDLE --AND THE BIRDS ATTAINING A SPEED OF **40** MILES PER HOUR

ROBERT BURTON
(1577-1640)
AUTHOR of "The ANATOMY of MELANCHOLY"
ACCURATELY PREDICTED THE EXACT
DATE OF HIS NATURAL DEATH
-- JANUARY 25, 1640 -
10 YEARS BEFORE HIS DEMISE

AN **ELEPHANT'S** GESTATION PERIOD VARIES WITH THE SEX OF ITS OFFSPRING -- **18 MONTHS FOR A FEMALE AND 22 MONTHS FOR A MALE**

THE **LESSER YELLOWLEGS** HAS A CRY THAT SOUNDS LIKE *"KEEP-A-GOING, KEEP-A-GOING"*

THE **"BAIKAL"**
A COMBINATION FERRY AND ICEBREAKER
BUILT IN NEWCASTLE-UPON-TYNE, ENGLAND, IN 1896, WAS DISASSEMBLED
AND SHIPPED IN THOUSANDS OF PARTS TO LAKE BAIKAL, IN SIBERIA
-- A JOURNEY BY SHIP, RAIL AND RIVER BARGE OF 7,000 MILES

| OBEDIAH DIED SEPT. 28, 1805 AGE 7 MONTHS | OBEDIAH DIED JULY 10, 1811 AGE 4 YEARS | OBEDIAH DIED AUG. 10, 1812 AGE 28 DAYS |

EPITAPHS OVER THE GRAVES OF 3 SUCCESSIVE
SONS OF JENNET CRANE -- *WHO VAINLY
SOUGHT TO PERPETUATE THE NAME OBEDIAH*
FIRST PRESBYTERIAN CHURCHYARD, ELIZABETH, N.J.

THE **BARBARY DEER** FOUND IN ALGERIA AND TUNISIA *IS THE ONLY SPECIES OF DEER IN ALL AFRICA*

THE **BARN OWL** of Jamaica *SWALLOWS MICE, BIRDS AND LIZARDS WHOLE*

THE **CATHEDRAL** of **ST. VINCENT** IN BERNE, SWITZERLAND, WORK ON WHICH WAS STARTED IN 1421, WAS NOT COMPLETED UNTIL 1893 --472 YEARS LATER

EARTHENWARE JARS INSCRIBED WITH WISHES FOR A FRAGRANT NEW YEAR WERE USED IN ANCIENT EGYPT AS NEW YEAR'S CARDS

SHOE In Tibet WITH A *BUILT-IN SHOE HORN*

THE **RED-VENTED BULBUL** of Ceylon CONTINUOUSLY CHIRPS WHAT SOUNDS LIKE " CHEEK BY JOWL "

ROGUE ELEPHANTS OFTEN RELIEVE THEIR LONELINESS BY ADOPTING A BIRD *WHICH RIDES ON THE PACHYDERM'S BACK*

THE **DRONE FLY** *HAS 20,000 EYES* EACH OF ITS 2 EYES HAS 10,000 OMMATIDIA --*EACH OF WHICH IS A COMPLETE VISUAL ORGAN*

THE **TOMBSTONE** of JULES BLEDSOE
FAMED SINGER WHO INTRODUCED
" OLD MAN RIVER"
BEARS THE NOTES AND WORDS
OF A LINE OF THE SONG:
"*HE JUST KEEPS ROLLING ALONG*"
Oakwood Cemetery, East Waco, Texas

THE **CHURCH** of **SAN BRUNO** in Italy
WAS WRECKED BY AN EARTHQUAKE IN
1783, EXCEPT FOR THE FAÇADE WHICH
REMAINED INTACT *ALTHOUGH THE
FINIALS ATOP EACH END WERE TURNED
COMPLETELY AROUND BY THE
FORCE OF THE QUAKE*

A **CUCKOO
CLOCK**
OWNED BY MRS.
PEARL DRUCKER
OF MONTEREY
PARK, CALIF.,
WHICH HAD NOT
WORKED FOR YEARS
WAS STARTED BY THE
RECENT CALIFORNIA
EARTHQUAKE
--AND HAS BEEN
KEEPING PERFECT
TIME EVER SINCE

THE FIGUREHEAD
ON THE NORWEGIAN
SHIP "BONNARD"
WAS DESIGNED BY
SCULPTOR ORNULFF BAST
AND IS A MOSAIC
*COMPRISING 25,000
PIECES OF BYZANTINE
RAVENNA GLASS*

PELET
de la
LOZÈRE
(1759-1842)
THE FRENCH
REVOLUTIONARY
LEADER WAS
ELECTED TO
THE FRENCH
LEGISLATURE
NOT ONLY BY
HIS OWN DISTRICT
OF LOZÈRE--BUT
*ALSO IN 70
OTHER DISTRICTS
WHICH HE WAS
NOT ELIGIBLE
TO REPRESENT*

THE VOLCANIC ERUPTION THAT WIPED OUT AN AMERICAN SUMMER!

THE TEMBORO, A VOLCANO IN INDONESIA, ERUPTING IN 1815, CHANGED CLIMATIC CONDITIONS THROUGHOUT THE WORLD GIVING THE UNITED STATES IN 1816 *"THE YEAR WITHOUT A SUMMER"* FRUIT TREES DID NOT RIPEN IN THE U.S., BIRDS DID NOT CHIRP, GRAIN DID NOT GROW, AND SNOW FELL IN JULY

CHORDOSPARTIUM STEVENSONII

A FLOWERING SHRUB GROWS ONLY IN ONE FIELD ON SOUTH ISLAND N.Z. --AND NOWHERE ELSE IN THE WORLD

GEORGE ROBERT TWELVE HEWES (1742-1843) TOOK PART IN THE BOSTON TEA PARTY IN 1773 AT THE AGE OF 31 *AND ATTENDED INAUGURATION OF THE BUNKER HILL MONUMENT* **70 YEARS LATER**

THE PICASSO TRIGGERFISH IS SO CALLED BECAUSE ITS COLORING LOOKS LIKE A DESIGN CREATED BY *PABLO PICASSO*

THE CONTRACT WITH A PENALTY CLAUSE THAT PROVED FATALLY PROPHETIC!

GASPARE BOELINI IN SELLING HIS CASTLE IN MESOCCO, SWITZERLAND, IN 1525 WAS SO CERTAIN THE TRANSACTION WOULD BE CONSUMMATED THAT HE SAID HE WOULD *STAKE HIS LIFE ON IT*— WHEN BOELINI LATER ATTEMPTED TO BREAK THE CONTRACT A SWISS COURT SENTENCED HIM TO BE *HURLED TO HIS DEATH FROM THE WALLS OF HIS OWN CASTLE*

THE **NEST** OF THE NEW ZEALAND HUMBLEBEE CONSISTS OF WAX CELLS, EACH CONTAINING ONE EGG --AND AS EACH BEE EMERGES ITS EMPTY CELL IS RE-UTILIZED FOR *THE STORAGE OF HONEY*

STANLEY PALACE in Chester, England, WAS LEASED TO THE CITY FOR 999 YEARS AT AN ANNUAL RENTAL OF *ONE PEPPERCORN* (1931)

MARY H. KILBORN
WIFE OF BYRON
OF MILWAUKEE
DIED AT HURON IN 1837
AGE 36 YEARS.
IN A COFFIN OF
ICE CONVEYED TO
WORTHINGTON, OHIO
AND THERE ENTOMBED.

EPITAPH in Center Cemetery, in East Granby, Conn., *OVER AN EMPTY GRAVE*

THE SIERRA SODA STRAW A PLANT FOUND IN OWENS VALLEY, CALIFORNIA, HAS HOLLOW STEMS WHICH MAKE EXCELLENT *SODA STRAWS*

LITCHI NUTS ARE NOT NUTS THEY ARE DRIED FRUIT